SOULSHIFT

SOULSHIFT

the measure of a life transformed

Steve DeNeff | David Drury

wesleyan
publishing
house

Indianapolis, Indiana

Copyright © 2011, 2012
Published by Wesleyan Publishing House
Indianapolis, Indiana 46250
Printed in the United States of America
ISBN: 978-0-89827-697-8

The Library of Congress has catalogued a previous edition as follows:

DeNeff, Steve.
  SoulShift : the measure of a life transformed / Steve DeNeff and David Drury.
    p. cm.
  Includes bibliographical references (p.).
  ISBN 978-0-89827-476-9
  1. Christian life--Wesleyan authors. I. Drury, David. II. Title. III. Title: Soulshift.
  BV4501.3.D457 2011
  248.4--dc22
                              2010042221

All royalties from sales of this book are donated by the authors to the nonprofit *SoulShift* work of College Church of Marion, Ind., as it resources other churches in restoring the future.

SOULSHIFT

A *SoulShift* church resource from College Church in
partnership with Wesleyan Publishing House

Go to wesleyan.org/wph/soulshift or CollegeWes.com
for more *SoulShift* resources.

CONTENTS

ACKNOWLEDGEMENTS

We've dreamed of what could happen if the people of our church were given the opportunity to resource other churches. Like the boy ready to share his lunch of loaves and fishes, we think God has given us something he wants us to share. *SoulShift* is our attempt to pass that lunch around. However, only God can bless and multiply it for you and your church. Our thanks first to our Lord for every mercy and opportunity he has provided. It is more than we deserve, even the very little we bring to the table.

THE AUTHORS WOULD BOTH LIKE TO THANK . . .

The leaders and volunteers in our church. *SoulShift* came out of community. We have written books before but never with so many contributing. For more than a year, dozens from College Church were involved by praying, brainstorming, experimenting, testing, rewriting, and editing. All their names could be put on the cover of this book. Thank you all for your humility, intelligence, and patience.

Our ministry leadership staff. You'll find their spiritual fingerprints all over this book. Thanks to Judy Huffman, Thad Spring, Emily Vermilya, Clif Davis, Jil Mazellan, Julia Hurlow, Matt Beck, Joel Liechty, and Mark Shepherd. Thanks for the creativity and ownership.

Thanks to Dan Swartz, Rhonda Conrad, Anne Bainbridge, Jackie White, Cindy Buck, G. B. McClanahan, and several other leaders whose hard work on *SoulShift* is helping facilitate a real spiritual movement in our church.

The elders and deacons of College Church. They helped craft this spiritual change dynamic early on while guiding, correcting, praying, and always encouraging us along the way.

Professors and leaders from Indiana Wesleyan University (IWU) and Wesley Seminary at IWU who are a part of our church. We are both indebted to them theologically and for countless personal reasons.

Professors and leaders from Taylor University who are a part of our church. They formed a small group to test drive *SoulShift* before publication, and they gave us real-world, practical feedback and some conceptual tweaking that improved it. We're grateful.

Many senior saints in our church. They contributed by sharing from their long experiences in making shifts of the soul. A handful of them joined that great cloud of witnesses in heaven while this was being written—this is a part of their immense legacy in the kingdom.

Wesleyan Publishing House has been a keen working partner for our church. The entire team there deserves a thank you, but in particular we're indebted to the big-thinking and hard-working efforts of Don Cady, Craig Bubeck, Kevin Scott, and Joe Jackson.

Even if it comes out of community, a book cannot be written by committee. That task fell to us as authors. Where this work proves to be biblical, practical, and inspirational, we can thank the above people. Any errors, omissions, or overstatements remain our own.

STEVE WOULD LIKE TO THANK . . .

The people of our church. They are my mentors, my colleagues, sometimes even my defenders—but always my friends, never just an audience. The leader of any church is less important than the church of any leader. Success depends upon the permission of the people led. So thank you, dear people of College Church, for granting me that permission the past ten years.

And thanks to David Drury, my coauthor on this project. Two people writing a book is like three people having a baby—sooner or later someone has to take charge. Dave has done that by weaving together his writings and mine into a manuscript that complements both styles. If something you read here makes sense, it is likely because Dave has found a way to keep it in the context of the greater goal. What doesn't make sense is quite possibly a part of my own writing that just could not be saved.

Thanks finally to my family, all of them, for bearing with my absent-mindedness, my neglect of details around the home, and my distant stares in conversations while I was mulling over something that would show up later in this book. The emphasis here, on genuine transformation, reflects a priority that was bred into me by my parents, who still pray every day for my family and ministry. My wife, Lori, has modeled many of the Soul-Shifts and, at times, even waited for me to catch up. Together we have watched God develop them in the lives of our kids, Nicholas and Ashley, and this has been our greatest joy.

DAVID WOULD LIKE TO THANK . . .

My partners in prayer. I currently have fifty-three very intentional inter-cessors on my prayer warrior team, and the strength I draw from them is intensely real and immensely encouraging.

I owe a great deal to Steve DeNeff, and especially for his trust in me as we pastor and lead together in our church community. Our trust only increased as we worked together to present some of Steve's most trans-forming spiritual insights in this book. Of course, he is only so trusting because he trusts Christ so much. I admire that and thank him for it.

Dr. Tim Steenburg advised me well and is hard at work developing a *SoulShift* assessment tool.

Rev. John Heavilin read and reread the early manuscript to help improve it.

Rev. Marcel Lamb lent me his keen pastoral eyes early.

My favorite theologian happens to be my brother, John Drury, and I hope his deep love of talking about God is rubbing off on me.

My personal thanks to Max Lucado and Karen Hill for taking a risk on me when I joined the Lucado team several years ago. Karen is a real maestro, and Max is the real deal. Their encouragement is silver, and their example is gold.

My family deserves heartfelt thanks. Maxim, Karina, and Lauren: God is shaping your souls already; nothing fills my joy meter more than you. Kathy, love of my life: thank you for the dozens of little adjustments you made as this book was on my mind and heart for so long and for the huge adjustment being my bride has been all along.

PREFACE

WE WANT TO BE DIFFERENT, BUT WE DON'T WANT TO CHANGE

Are you tired of people kicking sand in your face?"

Was I ever!

"And do you wish you could stand up to them?"

Yup.

"Let me prove I can make you a new man!"

He had me.

It was an advertisement in the back of a comic book. Wearing a leopard-skin swimsuit, the bodybuilder Charles Atlas promoted his new weight-training program for wimps. A cartoon showed a beach bully grabbing a scrawny kid and saying, "Listen here! I'd smash you in the face . . . only you're so skinny you might blow away." The scrawny kid's girlfriend taunted him, "Oh, don't let it bother you, little boy." I (Steve) will never forget that. I was thirteen years old.

Just like the scrawny kid in the comic, I was getting sand kicked in my face. Bullies would cut in front of me in the lunch line. I was tired of getting run over in the hall, tired of losing every wrestling match in gym class, tired of Coach Smiley (my gym teacher who never smiled) ridiculing my torso. But what was I to do? I couldn't help that I had grown so fast that I was all skin and bones, lanky and awkward. I was the scrawny kid on the beach (minus the girlfriend). My arms were as thick as a garden hose. My knees were knobby and my chest concave. My ribs stuck through my skin like bars on a xylophone.

But thanks to my new friend Charles Atlas, no bully was going to steal my girl—if I ever got one. Atlas was going to make a new man out of me.

The weight-training book was supposedly free, but I didn't believe it. Some of my friends had been snookered by these things before, so my best friend and I created a weight-training program of our own. We worked out five days a week. We ate wheat fiber pancakes and drank raw egg shakes. We wore weighted ankle bracelets. We even did isometric exercises in our chairs at school. Very gradually, it paid off. At the ripe age of sixteen, I was bench-pressing two hundred fifty pounds, curling eighty, and military pressing one hundred twenty. Not terribly impressive, I know, but I was betting it was more than Smiley at least. The trouble was that you couldn't tell. My arms went from a garden hose to vacuum hose. My thighs increased to the size of my knees and my ribs still looked like a xylophone. When I wore my tank top muscle shirt, my sisters called it a bone shirt. One of my friends said I could pose for Atlas weight-training program . . . as the before picture.

For three years, I had lifted those weights and had little to show for it. However, my best friend did. He developed a fifty-two-inch chest and twenty-three-inch arms, all hung on a six-foot-eight-inch frame. He was massive. He was hitting home runs; I was still hitting doubles. He got bigger; I got slightly stronger. But I wasn't lifting weights to get stronger; I lifted them to look better.

I felt cheated. Charles Atlas, with his chiseled body and leopard-skin swimsuit, had promised to make a new man out of me. No matter how much weight I lifted or how many eggs I ate, I did not look like Charles Atlas. Bullies were still taking cuts, and Smiley was still laughing at my torso. What good was that? So, I quit lifting. I am what I am, I decided. Only, I could never get myself to believe it. In the years that followed, I would try again. Then quit again. Then try again. This went on for years. In fact, I never gave up wanting to look better. But I gave up believing I could change.

Have you ever made a New Year's resolution to lose weight or get organized or spend more time with your family? Have you promised yourself that you would finish that degree or pay off that debt or fix up the house only to fall back again into the same old mess?

Diet and exercise websites experience a strong upsurge in hits during the first week of every year, reflecting our collective desire to change. Millions of people make New Year's resolutions to get skinny and in shape, but for most, the resolve is short-lived. Researcher Bill Tancer says, "By the fifth day of January, visits to dieting sites begin a steep slide that won't show any increases until summer, when there will be renewed dieting interest [in time] for bathing suit season."[1] The reason is that "we are a society that is increasingly fixated on finding instant gratification," says Tancer.[2] Anything that takes an inordinate amount of time is out of sync with everything else in our microwave-speed lives. But we remain compelled by instinct to make commitments to get better. At times, we are prompted by seeing a virtue in someone else. Other times, a crisis wakes us up, and we emerge with a new commitment to change something about ourselves. We want to be different, even if we seem to lack the tenacity to make it happen.

The same holds true with spiritual things. We want to be different in the way we know God. We want to have different attitudes. We want a different approach to the temptations we face. We commit to all kinds of spiritual activities, the spiritual versions of my teenage weight-training program, in hopes of being spiritually different. However, most of us never develop a clear image of what it means to be different. I had a relatively clear picture at age thirteen (thanks to Mr. Atlas) of what I wanted my body to look like. But I had a somewhat fuzzy picture, even at age thirty, of what I wanted my soul to look like.

By the age of thirty, I knew only that I wanted to quit sinning and be closer to God. Apparently, I was not alone. Research has shown that fewer than one in five of those who call themselves "born again" have any measurable goals for spiritual growth.[3] Many reported that their goal was to "become a better Christian" or "to grow spiritually." However, they did not—in fact, could not—define what this meant. Researcher George Barna writes, "We found that six out of ten believers have no sense of what they want to achieve or become, and roughly two out of ten have only the vaguest idea."[4] The dilemma is not that Christians aren't interested in spiritual growth or that they aren't willing to pay the price, but that they have only a limited and narrow understanding of what spiritual growth really means. They have never defined the target.

We can't blame individuals too much for this. While 95 percent say that their church encourages spiritual growth, less than half say that it "is one of the two or three highest priorities in their church."[5] About the same number (less than half) say that their church has communicated spiritual goals or established some standard expectations for the church. Only one out of five said that their church has some means of evaluating the spiritual maturity of the congregation.[6]

Jesus commissioned us to make disciples of all nations. But apparently, we're not entirely sure how to do that. Believers might say that their church encourages spiritual growth, but the statistics show that by this they only mean their church doesn't get in the way. Ironically, most of those who said that their church has not identified a clear path of discipleship, also said that they "would welcome any advice that the church might have for growing spiritually," and even that they would likely "pursue the changes suggested to them."[7]

That's why we've written this book. *SoulShift* is a clear and measurable way of defining the target for spiritual transformation. It differs from most discipleship programs in that it clearly identifies what it means to be a disciple in every area of life. Most programs tell you how to get started but never bother to tell you where you're going. Most spiritual growth resources stress ever-increasing discipleship inputs. They are often "to-do list" oriented. You have to read this daily or do that monthly or work with this person or go to that session. They are all good behaviors, no doubt, and perhaps quite helpful. But all this activity may leave you wondering, "How much is enough?" and "What am I trying to become with all my religious activity?"

Instead of focusing on inputs, *SoulShift* is an outcome-based, down-to-earth approach to your spirituality. You can enter this spiritual transformation process at any stage of life. You will be empowered to engage in seven shifts that will change your life — and keep changing it.

We hope this gives you an alternative to plug-and-play spirituality. Our dream is that it will help you to connect the dots of what might seem like random acts of disconnected spirituality in your life. We want you to make sense of it all and to actually see spiritual progress. By engaging with *Soul-Shift*, you will know exactly where you're going and how to get there.

This outcome-based approach is crucial because our human instinct to be different has competition. We have an opposing instinct that is just as compelling. We may want to be different, but we also want to quit becoming different when it gets difficult. We want to be different, but we don't want to change.

We wrote this book for people just like that — for people who have tried hard to be different but feel they haven't changed as much as they ought. It's for people who know what they should do but have trouble doing it. It's for those who have that one nagging sin that seems to float over them like a ghost.

That's not the way God wants it. Jesus didn't die on the cross so that we could all have more guilt in our lives. He died so we might be free.

INTRODUCTION

More than half a million people have heart-bypass surgery in America every year. Most are told that surgery is only a temporary fix; that the only long-term solution is a change in lifestyle and diet; that exercising, losing weight, and quitting smoking will increase their chance at living. Such advice is perhaps never more welcome and effective than when a person has had such a near-death experience. Instead, after one year, more than 90 percent of heart-bypass surgery patients report that they have not changed their lifestyle. Like most of us, they want to be different, but they don't want to change.

Janet Polivy, a sociology professor at the University of Toronto, has called our "persistent attempts at change despite previous failures" the false hope syndrome.[1] Our attempts to be different, she says, offer a sense of control and of at least being good enough to recognize the need for change, even if those feelings are misleading.

Many people settle in the land of compromise—not as bad as they once were but not as good as they had hoped to be. Some live their whole lives there, where promises and dreams decline.

The same land of compromise is populated by millions of Christians who have said similar things about their spiritual lives. They continue to battle with two instincts. One is to make promises, to decide to be different. The other is to quit, to decline to make the changes needed to really be different. These two instincts play themselves out in every new job, church, and relationship in our lives. What is at the bottom of this dilemma? Maybe the motivation to be different is misdirected.

The motivation to change is often based on a belief about how we will look in the future. Just as I (Steve) felt discontent with myself and imagined my future, complete with impressive Charles Atlas–style muscles, some people are discontented with their spiritually scrawny selves. They dream of being spiritually strong. They're so motivated by their dream that they will do, buy, and read anything to get better.

Too often, people are motivated by external things, rather than internal things. They don't just want to get stronger; they want others to know about it. They don't want to be more spiritual; they want others to see them as more spiritual. So they begin a series of actions designed to help them be different—to create a new version of themselves. They start disciplines, break habits, make new friends, and force themselves to engage in activities that are unnatural for them—the spiritual equivalent to lifting weights and eating raw eggs. They do this believing they will get immediate results. When all of their hard work fails to quickly produce the desired results, they stop trying. I am what I am, they decide. But the instinct to be different remains despite the instinct to quit.

Here is the vital difference between being *trans*formed and being *re*formed. Reformation usually has these three characteristics: (1) it comes from a voice on the outside; (2) it begins with a series of actions; and (3) it expects immediate results. But transformation by God's Holy Spirit works in exactly the opposite way: (1) it comes from a voice on the inside; (2) it begins with a change deep in our souls; and (3) it patiently waits for the results to show.

Transformation is a miracle, but it is not magic. It doesn't happen in an instant. It isn't easy or fun to watch. It doesn't defy logic. Sins don't disappear overnight. And we don't pull new virtues out of thin air. If you have tried many times to be different but haven't changed, if you feel defeated by the same old sin, or if God feels more distant than before, take heart! Don't quit. God has not given up on you. Don't give up on yourself.

Begin again. Only this time, ask God to change you into a different person. Don't make him a bunch of promises. Don't say that you will get control of your life. It's not about quitting everything cold turkey. It is better if you come to him with nothing—nothing but your frustration. It is better to come broken and bankrupt.

Ask God to reveal to you the true condition of your soul. Don't worry. He won't dump it all on you in one day. But you cannot discover it on your own. Only the Holy Spirit can probe the depths of your soul and reveal it to you. However, the Spirit will not invade you without being asked. You must ask him to come in, even daily.

There's a *Peanuts* comic where Charlie Brown said, "Sometimes I lie awake at night, and I ask, 'Where have I gone wrong?' Then a voice says to me, 'This is going to take more than one night.'" The process of peering into your soul will take much longer than one night.

As you tour the interior of your soul with God, tell him that you are sorry for all of the things about you that you cannot change, and name them. Grieve every one. Then, when you are through, get up out of your ashes and humbly say that you will begin again.

⟵⟶

For change to be genuine, there must be changes made in the soul. We who came into this world wired one way must go through a series of changes at the soul level until we leave this world wired another way. We call each change a SoulShift, and each is a seismic change deep in our being. They are far below the surface so that no one can see them at their start. They are like the earth's tectonic plates—always moving, always shifting, but rarely do people on the surface think about them.

Only when there is a major shift in tectonic plates do they alter anything on the surface. Earthquakes have the power to completely change the landscape. People who were once unaware of the shifting plates are confronted with evidence that is real and overwhelming. In a similar way, a SoulShift is a mostly subtle, sometimes revolutionary change that God makes on the interior of our lives and which alters everything else about us—from our habits to our personality to our tastes and preferences.

A SoulShift is not typically an abrupt change ushered in by a simple decision to follow Christ. These changes happen later. They begin in a day—sometimes in a moment—but they are not completed in that moment. They are often reflected in an action, but they are not the same as that action. They are deeper than that. They are movements or evolutions. Sometimes they are as dramatic as an earthquake and at other times as subtle as the rising of the sun. Sometimes they are evident to everyone, and sometimes they are evident to no one but God and us. But what all of these shifts have in common is this: They are deeper and even more permanent than a habit; they have repercussions that take time to work out; and they are a turn away from our culture toward the culture of Christ. They disentangle us from the world even as we remain in it. Yes, they affect the way we act, but they are more about the way we are wired. Embracing a Soul-Shift is a major step forward for those who want to be different but don't want to change.

In this book, we address seven shifts that will help you move beyond wanting to be different to experiencing genuine change:

1. Me to You is a shift in orientation from focusing on ourselves to focusing on others.

2. Slave to Child is a shift in identity from serving God to loving God.

3. Seen to Unseen is a shift in values from embracing things that are temporary to embracing things that are eternal.

4. Consumer to Steward is a shift in ownership from acquiring things for ourselves to offering what we have to God and others.

5. Ask to Listen is a shift in posture from asking others to listening to God.

6. Sheep to Shepherd is a shift in influence from following the crowd to leading like Christ.

7. Me to We is a shift in priority from individualism to community.

We have been asked many times why there are only seven shifts and not twelve or three, since these numbers are equally important in the Bible. Actually, we considered using the biblical number forty, or even 144,000, but it seemed like a lot of work. Seriously, we have tried to cover as broad a spectrum as seems wise for a person to engage in, aiming to be comprehensive but not cumbersome. These are seven of the most crucial and often neglected changes that must be made in a transformed life.

However, we do not pretend that this is an exhaustive list. You might have three or four that you're thinking of right now. This is only a way to get started. But we do believe that growth in these seven areas could mean, for most of us, a very different kind of life. We also don't pretend to have invented these areas of transformation. As you will see, they are found everywhere in Scripture and have been the core of how people change to become like Christ ever since Christ himself walked on the earth.

At the same time, *SoulShift* is no ordinary discipleship program. It's not a mold of some spiritual Charles Atlas that you're supposed to squeeze into, no leopard-skin swimsuit and no beach full of people to impress. Instead, each one of the shifts looks different when you lay it over your personality. For instance, if God has made you passive or introverted, you will still need to move from being a Sheep to Shepherd, but you will lead in a different way and always within the sphere of influence God has already given you. The shift from Consumer to Steward will look quite different for a teenager than it will for a corporate executive. And for one who was raised by abusive parents, the shift from Slave to Child will be much more difficult and dramatic, even more important, than for someone who had loving parents who affirmed them. Each shift is made within your life—the only one you have—not someone else's. In fact, you're already making these shifts in your life in many ways, but maybe you just didn't know what to call them.

A SoulShift is like baking bread. As a shift rises in your life, it performs the function of the yeast. It's not the pan. It doesn't force you into a mold that you got from someone else (the pan); it is the catalyst (the yeast) of the future you. It takes the form of whatever culture or of whatever circumstance you are in, and it blends with your personality and causes you to rise to your potential in Christ.

By beginning with the future you in mind, it might seem daunting. You'll need a starting point. The way to begin is to partner with what God's Spirit is already doing. As he walks around the interior of your life looking at the problems but also at your potential, you must work in tandem with him by choosing the forces that influence you. He will work in, and you must work out (Phil. 2:12–13)—always in that order.

≈

Now, imagine another photo, not of Charles Atlas, but of you. Imagine that God has a refrigerator in heaven with your picture on it. It's not a picture of you ten or twenty years ago. It's more like a photo of you ten or twenty years from now. Imagine that! God knows the future you. It's not about your outward appearance. His picture shows what's inside you—what motivates you, what your fears are, what dreams you've achieved, and what hopes you still have. Imagine what this shift in your life could look like.

Imagine if every morning when you woke up, your first instinct was to do what is right. And you loved it. That one nagging sin that you just can't get over? It's gone. You're not going to commit it today, and you know this. Remember how you always defended yourself or compared yourself when certain people were in the room? Gone! Now you have confidence. You're happy with who God made you to be. You don't worry whether your stock is rising or falling in the eyes of others, trying to please people constantly. You can accept criticism and not have it define you.

Imagine being just as concerned about other people—about their marriage, kids, or job—as you were once concerned about yourself. Imagine not wanting someone else to make the last out in the softball game or going to a basketball game and empathizing with the refs. Who does that?

Imagine knowing the will of God so well that you don't have to ask all the time. What if the Bible became the most relevant thing in your life? When you read it, another voice would speak out from within its pages, and it would make perfect sense to you. Imagine not running to the priest or the bookstore or the counselor to know what to do because you have heard from God himself when you were by yourself.

Imagine living on a fraction of your income and still feeling that it was plenty, and then using the rest for something bigger than you? What if you suddenly made plenty of money, and you never got a raise, and you used less of everything you always use.

Imagine praying twenty times as much as you do now and doing it because you like to, not because you had to, just as you like hanging out with your best friends. And what if your heart was broken by things that break the heart of God? What if you could see, with your mind's eye, a whole new set of realities that were invisible to everyone else but just as real—even more real—than everything around you?

Imagine what all this might be like, with your soul shifted toward God in every way.

Last month, I (Steve) conducted a funeral for a woman who died from brain cancer. A few hours before she passed, she opened her eyes and looked away, past those gathered around her bed. She then smiled and said, "I never knew." It was as though she was staring into something that was in the room, right next to her husband's head, but she was the only one who could see it. A moment later, as she gazed into that realm, she said, "I have so much to learn." And within a few moments, she was gone. Well, imagine if you learned much of that in the next several years? Imagine knowing in this world the truths of the next one, because you can see it with the eye of faith.

This is the dream God has for you. It's the picture of the future you that he puts on his fridge. It's you—restored to his original plan. He's already at work restoring your future.

But where do you begin? What kinds of things should you infuse into your soul—your life—to change it? That's what this book is about. For the next seven chapters, we'll take a look at each SoulShift, unpacking what it means in the Bible and in life. We'll give examples of each with practical suggestions for how you can cooperate with what God is already doing.

Are you ready to shift?

SEVEN SOULSHIFTS

 ME TO YOU is a shift in orientation from focusing on ourselves to focusing on others.

We are wired, all of us, for self-preservation. From birth, our first struggles are selfish ones. So the shift from thinking primarily about me (yourself) to thinking primarily about you (others) is one of the most fundamental shifts we will make. Indeed, the whole world is different when we see it through the eyes of someone else. Once we've shifted from Me to You, the horizons of life expand infinitely because we no longer see ourselves as the point. (See pages 31–45.)

SLAVE TO CHILD is a shift in identity from serving God to loving God. We are consumed with laws, sin, judgment, serving God, and getting crowns in heaven. We lack confidence in our relationship with God. We wonder if we can do this or that and still be a Christian. We worry we've crossed the line. When we shift from this kind of slavery and realize we are God's children, everything changes. Instead of just serving God, we are concerned with pleasing him (Eph. 5:10). We are no longer just doing God's will; we have God's mind (1 Cor. 2:16). We accept our identity as children of God and live with all of the privileges and responsibilities that come with it. (See pages 47–60.)

3 **SEEN TO UNSEEN** is a shift in values from embracing things that are temporary to embracing things that are eternal.

We are born into a tangible world that we can touch, smell, see, and feel. But right next to our heads—as close as the air we breathe—is a kingdom that is eternal and invisible. Over time, God will teach us how to see a kingdom that, although invisible, is approaching with unnerving speed. God wants us to learn to see now what we will have no problem seeing after we are in heaven. Things we once considered unimportant will have a new urgency, and things we once valued might become more trivial. (See pages 61–71.)

4 **CONSUMER TO STEWARD** is a shift in ownership from acquiring things for ourselves to offering what we have to God and others.

Our souls may be saved, but we are still consumers. We complain about our salaries, fatten our retirements, stockpile more than we can use, and then want more. Over time, the Holy Spirit will change us into being stewards who see that all we have is only borrowed from God. We will become less attached to things and more generous. We will no longer measure life in terms of possessions. And we won't even miss them when they're gone. (See pages 73–88.)

5 **ASK TO LISTEN** is a shift in posture from asking others to listening to God.

We look outside of ourselves for answers—to sermons and books, seeking advisors to tell us exactly what to do. We worry about missing the will of

God for our lives. We read the Bible like a desk reference as though it should answer our questions. When we make this shift, rather than asking God or someone else to answer our questions, we begin to ask the questions God is already answering. We will let him speak. We will let him set the agenda. We will listen. (See pages 89–106.)

6 **SHEEP TO SHEPHERD** is a shift in influence from following the crowd to leading like Christ.

Most of us are quite good at following or we would not be Christians at all. But something happens when Jesus, who first asked us to follow him, then tells us to lead. The call to follow becomes the call to lead in the very circles in which we once followed. Our prayers become an intercession. To volunteer is to minister. Our careers become a calling and we, who were sheep, become shepherds. (See pages 107–123.)

7 **ME TO WE** is a shift in priority from individualism to community.

Something pivotal happens in our lives when we begin to accept the identity of our community. We seek counsel. We accept correction. We allow those around us to teach us about God and interpret him for us. We use our talents and develop our gifts according to affirmation of others. In short, we find ourselves as Jesus said we would, by losing ourselves in the community of God. (See pages 125–140.)

ME TO YOU

**a shift in orientation from focusing on
ourselves to focusing on others**

There was only one skill I (Dave) still had to master to graduate from kindergarten: to tie my shoes. I could not master this art no matter how hard I tried. Mrs. Ward would have us all untie our shoes and hold them up for her to see, and then all our tiny heads would disappear under the tables to tie them again. I was the only child who didn't get it. I was terrified of flunking the grade. I imagined myself six years later, still stuck in kindergarten, sitting at a desk too small for me, all because of my untied shoes.

My solution came in the form of a brown-eyed girl who sat next to me in Mrs. Ward's class. I don't recall being romantically involved with her. However, I had pulled her pigtails a few times at recess, so that's sort of the five-year-old equivalent. When it was time for the last untied shoes drill of the year, I leaned over and stuck my untied feet under her desk when the teacher wasn't looking. No words were exchanged; none were needed. She had pity on me and tied my shoes, and by cheating, I graduated from kindergarten. Later in life, I earned my degrees and academic accomplishments, but if not for the brown-eyed girl, I might still be trying to pass kindergarten.

I wasn't the best behaved or brightest bulb in the bunch. I was way behind in learning math. My grandfather had taught me a silly little trick for addition that stuck in my head (to be honest, I still sometimes revert to it), and it messed me up all the time. I was frustrated at times—I once even got kicked off the bus for punching out another kid's tooth.

Into these early years came the most unwelcome addition I could imagine: a baby brother. Up until then, I had been the baby. But after that, all Mom's time seemed to go to the newcomer in the crib—the supposedly cute, little John. He would cry constantly. I didn't understand why in the world my parents would need another boy. They already had me!

One night, I snuck into John's room. I stood by the crib frowning down at him. I expected to see him sleeping. But baby John was wide awake and looked right back at me. Maybe I realized that John looked a little like me, and that changed my mind. Maybe he wasn't crying for the first time ever, and so I finally spent some time with him without being driven insane. Whatever it might have been, something selfish in me shifted, and I started to think differently about the newcomer.

One of my favorite stories back then was when Prince Jonathan gave his armor, bow, and sword to David. I thought that was pretty cool—giving someone you liked something that protected you and was one of the most important things you owned. I went back into my room and then snuck back to give baby John a present.

In the morning, my mom found baby John cuddling my favorite blankie—the same one I had used since I was months old. By that time, I had been hiding it under my pillow for a few years, so my friends wouldn't know that I slept with a special baby blanket. When Mom asked me how it got into John's crib, I said, "It's baby brother's blankie now. He needs it more than I do."

What would make a kid shift like that? It wasn't natural. I was born self-ish. That poor kid on a school bus with his tooth knocked out was proof. My cheating to graduate from kindergarten was further proof. It was all about me. But something small happened that started to shift my life from Me to You.

⤝

Sometimes it all seems to fall apart. Murphy's Law is in force, and rough times run rampant. These are the times when it's not just raining; it's pouring.

This was the case for a woman named Naomi. A horrible famine was rav-aging her country. More than a downturn in the economy or a recession in the markets, this food shortage was causing starvation. So, Naomi and her hus-band packed up and moved out. They became immigrants. After moving to the Middle-Eastern country of Moab, they were strangers in an even stranger land. But they were no longer in danger of starving. In fact, their sons even found wives in this new land. Naomi and her husband started to settle down, hopeful for grandchildren. It seemed like their luck had changed.

No such luck. When it rains, it pours. And when it pours, it sometimes turns into a hurricane of hurt.

It would get much worse before it got better. Naomi's husband died. This bitter grief quickly tripled when one of her sons died, followed by the other. All the men in the family—wiped out tragically too soon. Three wid-ows who barely knew each other were left behind: Naomi, Ruth, and Orpah. Naomi decided to go back home since the famine was passing. She reasoned that it would be better to be in poverty among her own people than to be an impoverished immigrant widow.

At first, it seemed that Ruth and Orpah, in loyalty to their widowed mother-in-law, would travel to Naomi's country with her. However, on the road home, the aging woman spoke to the young widows: "Go back, each of you, to your mother's home. May the LORD show kindness to you, as you have shown to your dead and to me. May the LORD grant that each of you will find rest in the home of another husband" (Ruth 1:8–9).

Even with this speech, the two Moabite widows resisted the permission to abandon their mother-in-law and said they would go on with her. She replied, "No, my daughters. It is more bitter for me than for you, because the LORD's hand has turned against me!" (1:13 TNIV).

At this, Orpah headed home, probably reasoning with herself the whole way: "Naomi's mind is made up, and she is going to meet her Maker without me. I offered to go with her, and she told me not to. I did all I could, right? Of course, I have a family back in Moab to return to. I have a chance—even if it's slim—to pick up the pieces of my life. Naomi's release is, in fact, a relief! It is perfectly understandable and expected for me to head home."

It's only natural, especially when you've hit rock bottom, to look out for yourself.

But Ruth threw a wrench into this rationale. As Orpah headed home, Ruth stayed, clinging to her mother-in-law (1:14). Naomi could see that this one was not listening to reason. I love the first word Naomi said to the misled young widow: "'Look,' said Naomi" (1:15).

Can't you just see a mother-in-law—hands on hips, cocking her head to the side—beginning her scolding sentence with "Look." You know a soapbox speech is about to come. You're going to get told how out of line you are when she starts with the word *look*.

Ruth looked up and listened to Naomi's last lecture: "Look . . . your sister-in-law is going back to her people and her gods. Go back with her" (1:15).

Not only did she pull out the look, but she also did the whole family-comparison thing. This was a major escalation. You know the kind: "Well, your sister does it this way" or "Your sister-in-law gets this, so why don't you?" Naomi raised the stakes. Multiple times Naomi tried to send Ruth home. Ruth just didn't get the picture. Why? Couldn't she take a hint? Did she need it spelled out for her on a flannel graph?

The Middle-Eastern dust must have muddled her mind. So here's how I (Dave) might have explained it more clearly to Ruth had I been there: "OK, Ruth. Poor, poor, Ruthie. You see, like Orpah, you have a family and some security back home in Moab. In Naomi's home country, you'll just be an outsider—an impoverished immigrant widow—like Naomi was in Moab. Being an outsider, it's going to be crazy hard for you to ever remarry. And remarriage is your only ticket to financial security in these ancient times. I'll let you in on a dirty little secret too: Naomi's people are pretty snobbish about intermarriage. And they're really big on the 'how many Moabites does it take to screw in a light bulb' jokes. It's just going to be awkward. Naomi is completely right. Why can't you see what's best for yourself, Ruth?"

Here's why: Ruth wasn't looking out for herself. She was looking out for Naomi. Ruth knew that while her chances of remarriage and a new secure life would be slim, Naomi's chances for the same were nil. She knew that Naomi was too old to work fields, remarry, and continue her line and hold on to any assets she had back home. She worried that her mother-in-law would die penniless and alone. Ruth's situation was hard, but instead of focusing on herself, she was selfless. She wasn't born that way. Nobody is. Something happened to Ruth. She had moved from Me to You.

We have a tendency to put ourselves first. We cut in line, whether in the elementary school lunchroom or the interstate merge lane. Children sit themselves in the middle of their toys and say, "Mine." Gangs have turf. Suburbanites have privacy fences. Nonverbally, we all say to others: No Trespassing!

Why are we inclined toward fighting, war, and competition? Why do we try to gain advantage? Why do we conspire and sabotage? Why do we compare ourselves with others? What makes one race develop prejudices against another, and what makes the other hate them for it and seek revenge? Why is power, violence, or conquest the first thing we think of when something goes wrong? Scripture has a three-letter answer for these questions: s-i-n. Selfishness might be the most basic of offenses—the most obvious one, even in a toddler. But the root of this selfishness is sin.

The Bible talks a good deal on this subject. Depending on the translation you use, the Bible talks about sin between five hundred and eight hundred times. Covering all of what Scripture says about sin would take an entire book. In the book of Romans alone, Paul talks about sin dozens of times.[1] March in a straight line through Romans and the scriptural sentries point to a clear definition of sin.

Where did sin come from? Romans 5:12 says it started with Adam: "Sin entered the world through one man, and death through sin, and in this way death came to all men, because all sinned." So, sin started there and causes death. Without sin, we would live on this earth forever. But why us? Why does the action of one man have such effects on us now? Since then, we "all have sinned and fall short of the glory of God" (Rom. 3:23). We are just as culpable as Adam. We are just as selfish. We all would have taken a bite out of that apple.

Our sin has consequences. As Romans 6:23 says, "the wages of sin is death." It's as if you work all week on something and then get a big paycheck of debt instead of money at the end of the week. Eugene Peterson put the same verse this way: "Work hard for sin your whole life and your pension is death" (MSG). Live a life of sin and all you get is a 401(k) of hellfire.

Does this really affect all of us? What about you? Me? Yes. "Basically, all of us, whether insiders or outsiders, start out in identical conditions, which is to say that we all start out as sinners. Scripture leaves no doubt about it" (3:9 MSG). This is not good news. Yes, we're all on this train together. But it's a one-way, nonstop ticket to torment.

The book of Romans has the good news about sin too. Because of what Christ has done, we can be free from this. We can jump the train and catch a ride in the other direction on the other track: "You have been set free from sin" (6:18). Instead of shaking our heads and bemoaning our dire destiny, we can count ourselves "dead to sin but alive to God in Christ Jesus" (6:11).

When the soul shifts its tracks toward God, each churn of the wheels delivers more freedom. You're moving farther from sin and death. The person born selfish, like Ruth, becomes selfless. It's a shift in the soul that can only be possible by Christ's sacrifice. You're right—it's not natural; it's supernatural.

❧

When we left the story of Ruth, she was clinging to her mother-in-law's skirt, not wanting to abandon her. Staring up sharply with fierce determination, Ruth said: "Don't urge me to leave you or to turn back from you. Where you go I will go, and where you stay I will stay. Your people will be my people and your God my God. Where you die I will die, and there I will be buried" (Ruth 1:16–17 TNIV).

So, the two widows crossed the border—the younger, selfless one serving the older, embittered one. Naomi's story reached a turning point in this moment. Blessing after blessing followed from Ruth's selflessness. The story for Ruth concluded with one of the better endings you could imagine for that impoverished immigrant widow, whose selflessness turned it all around. Not only did Ruth marry a charming, wealthy businessman, but her great-grandson, David, also became king of the country she immigrated to: Israel.

❧

We begin life curved inward toward ourselves, caring only about our own needs. The infant cries for the bottle, a teenager worries about how she looks, or an adult obsesses over his career. We are hardwired for self-preservation, self-advancement, and self-comfort. If you doubt this, pull out an old yearbook or a photo of a group you're in. Who do you look for first? Who do you worry most about not looking good? Or, if something bothers you when you go out—even when you go to church—whose interests and preferences drive your criticism? Don't worry, I'm like that too. I'm hardwired to be all about me.

I (Steve) went into a restaurant with a Christian man I'll call Jason who was very outspoken about his faith. He called the server over to tell her to "turn off that music; it's offensive to my Christian faith." I mused about this later because if she wanted to, the server could have said: "But sir, if you are truly Christian, it's not your preference that should most concern you, but those of the others here—and they haven't complained." The shift from thinking primarily about me to thinking primarily about you is to curve outward toward others, so that you see them first. You choose your career, spend your money, and pray for them first and yourself second. Instead of "What should I do with my life?" you ask "Where can I best serve others?" Instead of "Do I believe in that project enough to donate my money?" you ask "Does someone need my money more than me? And would it help them or hurt them if I gave it?" Even your prayer life changes from "Dear God, let's talk about me" to "Dear God, there's someone I'd like you to help."

Many years ago, when the members of the Salvation Army gathered for a conference, they were saddened to learn that their founder, William Booth, was too sick to come. Booth was expected to deliver the keynote address to the conference but was unable to travel. Instead, he asked if he could write his speech and have it read for him at the conference. The night came and the crowd gathered to hear their revered founder's speech read to them. They expected his words to explain many things, to inspire them with a rationale for their service.

Instead, Booth was able to fit his entire speech into one telegram message. It represented the focus of the movement's work. When the telegram was read to the crowd, it contained but one word: "Others."

That is what it is all about for those who have moved from Me to You. The heart of the shifted soul is broken by the needs of others, not the self.

The eyes of the shifted soul are constantly looking to the needs of others, not the self. What's Me to You about? In one word: *others*.

❦

It has been said that the final test of any religion is how it affects our relationships with other people. Our relationships serve as mirrors for the soul; they show us how spiritual we really are. When we read "Love the Lord your God . . . [and] love your neighbor as yourself" (Mark 12:30), we don't mind asking ourselves how much we love God because it's hard to measure. No one knows but you and God. But it gets much more uncomfortable when we ask ourselves how much we love others. However, the Ten Commandments, the Lord's Prayer, and the fruit of the Spirit all include the love of others, not just the love of God.

While we tend to assess ourselves first on the question about God and then the question about others, the Bible actually turns these around, assessing love for others prior to love for God (see 1 John 4:12–17, 20).

Do you want to know how much you love God? How much do you love the "other" in your life? How much do you give to the least, to the AIDS patient, to the poor, to the unemployed, to the oppressed, to the victim of tragedy, to the citizen whose nation is at war with us? How much energy do you put forth to love those who are least like you? How well do you forgive? How much do you overlook? How consistently do you defend? How committed are you to the person over the organization? How well do you transition people out when they can no longer perform? How well do you break up when the serious relationship is over? How well do you honor those with weird habits or annoying behaviors? How many chances do you give those who let you down?

Jesus sends us into the boardrooms where people haggle over power, into the families where the trust has been destroyed by broken promises, and into the boroughs of cities where people are wrapped up in their addictions. Jesus points toward the last vestiges of racism and unemployment, where men have been robbed of their dignity; to the nursing homes, where those who no longer seem useful to society are now marginalized; or to the hospitals, where patients sit quiet and afraid. He calls us to look into the hearts of such people and see the kingdom: What are their true needs? What help is still available to them? What is God's dream for them?

God's dream for you is to dream for them more than yourself — to act in such a way that their needs are met before your own, to be so selfless as to help before you hoard. He wants you to entertain others rather than yourself, to move from Me to You. Why? Your love for God is no greater than your love for others.

⤝

Beth recently turned fifty. No one at work knew it because as her fiftieth birthday approached, she told people several times that she was fifty-two. While some women lie and say they are younger than they are, Beth inflated her age so coworkers wouldn't make a big deal about her fiftieth birthday with the usual black balloons and jokes about her age. It was all a cover. In reality, she was freaking out. She didn't think she could handle a room full of people calling her old, even in jest.

Things were changing way too fast for Beth at work. The boss had hired three new salespeople who were nearly half her age. They knew all the technology as if they'd been born using it. She frequently checked her 401(k) accounts and even the retirement section in the company policy manual to make sure they couldn't force her out before she was ready. She couldn't believe how fast the years were passing by. It seemed like just yesterday she was the one with all the potential, the one breaking the glass ceilings and being admired by many.

Her office was right next to one of the new kids, a newlywed named Emma, who was fresh out of college at twenty-three years old. Beth had been surprised a few months earlier when Emma showed up at her Sunday school class at church. After politely chatting a few moments after class, she was mortified to learn that her husband, Jim, had been talking to Emma's husband and had arranged for all of them to go out to lunch together.

Over the meal, Emma confessed to Beth that she was a bit overwhelmed with the new job, and that she didn't quite know where to start. Over dessert, Emma's husband hinted that their first year of marriage had been a struggle—they had moved four times that first year, including short stints in both of their parents' basements. As she listened, Beth felt her heart shift slightly. She didn't know if it was indigestion or something more spiritual. Whatever the case, Beth looked at Emma differently after that. She began thinking to herself: "Maybe I could take this girl under my wing a bit. If she's looking for some advice at work and at home, maybe I should help her out." Rather than competing with Emma for the attention of others in the office, Beth began to dream of ways to help Emma succeed.

Beth and Emma started going to breakfast every Friday morning, and Emma began looking at Beth as her mentor.

The shift Beth was going through was the ongoing shift from Me to You. She had done many selfless things throughout her life, but this new phase of life—her fifties—offered new opportunities to become more like Christ, ones she had never faced before. Aging itself was part of the shift.

⤙

"May I sit here?" I (Steve) asked a middle-aged lady sitting in the campground cafeteria. Right next to her was a little girl, about four years old, slumped over her meal tray, frowning at her supper. She hadn't taken a single bite. She just rolled her eyes back and forth, while the lady next to her talked about the camp. The little girl's face said it all: "I hate this place."

Halfway through the meal, I thought I'd give a shot at cheering her up: "What are you eating there? Is that Jell-O? Oh man, I love Jell-O" (yes, I was stretching the truth a bit).

I kept on with my act, saying, "If you're not going to eat your Jell-O, then I think I will." As I reached out with my spoon, she chopped off a large bite with her fork and shoveled it into her mouth. I feigned a frown, and she giggled.

I was onto something. "What's that over there?" I said, pointing to the other side of her tray. "Is that meat? Holy cow, I love meat! While you're eating your Jell-O, I think I'll eat your meat." Again, before I could move, she stabbed it with her fork and threw it into her mouth. Now there was Jell-O and roast beef in there, rolling around together while she giggled. "Are those lima beans?" I asked. "You can't be serious! I dream about lima beans every night. You must hate those—every kid does—so I'm going to eat yours." You might not believe me, but this little girl even shoveled the lima beans into her mouth, along with the Jell-O and roast beef.

After this joking and encouragement, she ate her whole meal in just minutes. By the end of supper, we were friends. She asked if I was going to be there again tomorrow. "You're welcome to join us any time," the kind lady said. And so I did. The next day, I sat there again. I feigned the same interest in the little girl's supper, and she ate it again, right out from under me, laughing the whole time, showing me the chewed food inside her mouth. Day after day this went on.

The final evening of the camp, the kind lady approached me by herself. "I want to thank you for coming here this week and for preaching your heart out every night," she said. After pausing, she went on, "You said some great things, I'm sure, but to be honest with you, I can't remember much of what you said." Well, this compliment was going in a different direction than I had hoped. Then she explained why: "All I can remember are the meals when you sat with us and helped my granddaughter eat. Gosh, I don't think she would have eaten anything all week if you hadn't teased her about stealing her food."

She told me the rest of the story: "A few years ago, my son-in-law walked out on my daughter and their little one. My granddaughter hasn't had a daddy in her life since. Every summer, I ask if I can have her for a week so I can take her to this camp, and I pray every year that God will send someone into this little girl's life who will show her the love of God. This year, it was you. I want to thank you for allowing God to love her through you. You know, she hasn't heard a word you said in this sanctuary, but I am sure she will remember a tall, bald, nameless man who spent his suppers having fun and helping her to eat."

It was such a small thing. I didn't lead that little girl to Christ. I didn't heal any emotional wounds or find her a new daddy. All I did was goof around. Who knew that you could goof around and do the will of God?

I suspect it's because of something St. Francis of Assisi said hundreds of years ago. He told us to "Preach the Gospel at all times and when necessary use words."[2]

Some people might have thought my preaching was the most important thing that week. But it wasn't the words I used that mattered most. It was trying to steal a little girl's lima beans.

REFLECT AND WRITE

In what ways has God already made shifts in your soul from Me to You? Write your story and testimony of what God has done in you.

How might God be calling you to shift from Me to You in the coming year? Write how you have felt God leading you or what impressions you received from him during this chapter.

ME TO YOU QUESTIONS

The SoulShift questions are designed to help you find yourself on spiritual radar, rather than merely guessing where you are. There are three categories: (1) questions to ask yourself in reflection; (2) questions for a trusted friend or SoulShift coach to ask you; and (3) questions to discuss in a smaller group of people growing together spiritually. These questions were developed by the Ministry Leadership Team of College Church.

SOULSHIFT QUESTIONS YOU ASK YOURSELF

In a normal day, how much do you think of the opinions and needs of others?

What personal rights have you given up for the good of someone else?

What is something significant that you have done for someone other than yourself this week?

SOULSHIFT QUESTIONS YOU WILL NEED TO BE ASKED

If your closest friends or spouse were asked, what would they say about your willingness to care for others?

What evidence is there that God is making you more aware of the needs of people around you?

What habits have you developed that enable you to ignore others? How often do you build up that barrier?

SOULSHIFT QUESTIONS YOU WOULD DISCUSS WITH OTHERS

What are some things about this group that would make it easy for someone to join it? What about us might make it hard?

What plans do you have to work together in opening the door to others to join?

Think of a nonprofit organization that would benefit from a few hours of volunteer work. What is the organization? What kind of work do they need? What would it take for your whole group to volunteer there together?

2

SLAVE TO CHILD

**a shift in identity from
serving God to loving God**

The days are mostly uneventful in Grant County, Indiana, where we live. But one night, a fight erupted when a homeowner interrupted the pillaging of two men who had broken into his house. As the fight carried into the backyard, the robbers bashed the owner's head on concrete. The man survived the attack, but when he awoke twelve hours later, he didn't remember a thing.

You've probably heard amnesia stories before. Fiction books are full of them; many films revolve around them; and soap operas are ridiculed for using them so often as a plot device.

But this was real. This regular guy suddenly became a real-life Jason Bourne — waking up in a strange place and not knowing who he was or how he got there.

Imagine finding yourself in a similar situation.

You wake up with a massive headache with a woman you don't recognize by your side, yet she is caring for you like a soul mate. They bring a child for you to hold. You can see the resemblance, but you don't recall seeing this, your flesh and blood, ever before.

A bit later, a group of people flock into your room and begin praying for your recovery. You don't recognize a single face, yet they seem deeply concerned about you and your family.

You begin trying to remember anything—what you do for a living, where you live, where you were born—but your mind is a blank slate. You can't remember your phone number or e-mail address. You don't even remember that you're not supposed to touch a hot cookie sheet in the oven. You are like a traveler with no luggage. You're separated from your past, your network of relationships, and any memories that would connect your past to the present moment.

While the homeowner who was attacked eventually recovered from the horrible physical trauma, his recovery from the mental trauma was a different story. In facing the psychological battle of figuring out the thousands of details most of us assume about our own identity, he was forced to depend on the assistance of others.

His family helped him fill in many of the blanks. They began telling him, "Your name is Jeff, and we are your family. We love you. You're important to us, and you're not alone. Let us explain to you who you are. Right now, we know you better than you know yourself." They showed him pictures and told him stories and slowly began to paint a picture of the man he was before the assault and the man they hoped he would one day be again. Through their patient efforts, Jeff Brady began to realize his true identity.

Most of us will never go through the kind of mental trauma Jeff went through. We know our names. We know who we are. We don't need others to tell us our identity.

Or do we?

What if we are not who we think we are?

Each of us is surrounded by a cacophony of voices that say things like, "You are not good enough. You are not important. You are strange. You are unimpressive." Every time we fail at something—in business, religion, or relationships—our suspicion is reinforced: "I am a loser." But all the while, Christ is beside you saying, "You don't know who you really are, but I do." He says, "You have spiritual amnesia, and it will take some time for you to recover from it. But trust me. I know you better than you know yourself."

He tells you that your identity is found in him. He calls you pet names that are out of the ordinary—things like saint, temple, and fragrance. These are loaded nicknames, and it's difficult to wrap your mind around them. You tell Jesus who you think you are, and he tells you who you really are.

This concept of God giving us a new identity is one of the central themes of the Bible. From the beginning, God gave his people new names: Sarai became Sarah, Abram became Abraham, Jacob became Israel, Simon became Peter, and Saul became Paul. Each new name marks one of God's people with a new identity. In the book of Revelation, Jesus promises to write on us the name of God and his "own new name" (Rev. 3:12 NRSV). He even promises to hand to each believer a "white stone with a new name written on it, known only to him who receives it" (2:17). All the way through the Scriptures, God challenges the image we have of ourselves.

We don't think we're worth much. We don't value the body God has given us; he calls our bodies a temple where the Holy Spirit lives (1 Cor. 3:16).

We say we can't ask for much, that we should be as humble as slaves in a throne room; he says we can "approach the throne of grace with confidence" (Heb. 4:16).

We feel condemned for our sin; he says we are free—and that there is "no condemnation" for us in him (Rom. 8:1–2).

We figure we are stuck with our sins or dirty little habits; he says he chose us to "be holy and blameless in his sight" (Eph. 1:4).

We think we're living the same life we've always lived; he says our life is now "hidden with Christ in God" (Col. 3:3).

We feel empty; he says we're given "all the fullness" (Col. 2:9).

We say we're sinners; he says we're saints (Rom. 1:7; Phil. 1:1).

You might be saying, "OK, I get the point. I'm not who I thought I was. I've been wrong about so many things." Jesus says, "No, you've been wrong about everything."

You thought you were a citizen of this country, but your "citizenship is in heaven" (Phil. 3:20).

You thought you were timid and lazy, but he gave you a spirit of power, love, and self-discipline (2 Tim. 1:7).

You might stop this litany from the Lord and say, "But I thought—" Jesus interrupts, "Think again, my friend." He continues to explain who he is and who you are because of it.

If "I am the vine; [then] you are the branches" (John 15:5).

If I am the head, then you are a member of my body (1 Cor. 12:12–26).

If I am the Holy One, then you are my saint (Eph. 2:19; 4:12).

If I am the King of Kings, then you are my empowered ruler in my kingdom (Dan. 7:18, 27).

If I am the Lord of Hosts, then you are my soldier equipped with my armor (Eph. 6:10–18).

If I am the Creator, then you are my "workmanship, created in Christ Jesus to do good work" (2:10).

Stunned, there you sit. Indeed, we all sit, realizing that we've mistaken our identity for so long. All we can say is, "If only we had known. We thought of ourselves as spiritual slaves, but you apparently think of us as so much more."

Jesus says in return, "I no longer call you servants, because a servant does not know his master's business. Instead, I have called you friends, for everything that I learned from my Father I have made known to you" (John 15:15). Because of what you've done, you think you only have the right to be his slave. But he gives you the right to be his child (1:12).

George MacDonald says, "Those to whom God is not all in all, are slaves. They may not commit great sins; they may be trying to do right; but so long as they serve God, as they call it, from duty, and do not know him as their father, the joy of their being, they are slaves—good slaves, but slaves."[1] While duty is a driving force, even for good, it is not God's dream for us. But spiritual amnesia often forces us into a role we were not reborn for. We feel the consequences of this all the time. Those who don't know who they are have to guess along the way.

Do you ever notice yourself playing a role or not knowing why you're acting the way you do? It's because of this truth: When you don't know who you are, you act like someone you're not—a person who is less than you are meant to be. And it will be harder to live like that than being who you really are. Acting is always harder than being.

When all of this happens, a great robbery takes place. You rob yourself and the world of what you could have offered if only you had been who you were meant to be. What's worse, you rob God of the person he invented, the person he wanted to empower to serve the world. Remaining in a state of perpetual spiritual amnesia is like abducting the child of God—yourself. His child is taken away, and a slave sits there instead. The whole time, we thought that was all we could be—his servant.

⁂

Jesus told some famous stories, but few are as well-known as the prodigal son. It has been painted by artists, reenacted in theatres, danced in ballet, preached by pastors, and even sung by popular acts like the Rolling Stones, Kid Rock, and U2. Every time the prodigal son story is told, the moral is the same: Sinners can be forgiven; God still loves; prodigals get a second chance. Yet hidden inside this famous story is a plot even better than the one we know. First, the story. Then, the plot (Luke 15:11–32).

A man has two sons. Both of them work for their father on the farm until the younger son grows tired of his boring life. After thinking about it for some time, he marches into his father's room with a bold and presumptive demand. He says, "Dad, give me the share of your property that will belong to me."

By asking for his share of the inheritance, this self-absorbed kid entitled himself to his father's belongings and, at the same time, subtly suggested that his father was as good as dead. Can you imagine? All he wanted from his father was his money. Remarkably, the father did not get angry. Even though he was not obligated to give his son anything, the father graciously agreed. He evenly divided the inheritance and gave him his portion early. As soon as he had the money, the young man packed up and left home. Nobody knew why. Was he trying to find himself? Was he looking for freedom? The young man ditched his past for something more—something better.

He ended up in a faraway country, very different from the one he was from, and there he began to squander his wealth on parties. After a few wild and crazy months, the well was dry. There was no more money. And that's when the famine hit. The whole country whirled into an economic recession. The markets crashed. Unemployment was up around 20 percent, and this young man, who was still a stranger there, was the least likely to be hired.

But he got lucky. Someone offered him a job feeding their pigs. Day after day, he found himself sloshing around in the mud, feeding animals that he would never eat. The animals were eating better than he was. The way Jesus put it was pretty depressing: "He longed to fill his stomach with the pods that the pigs were eating, but no one gave him anything" (15:16 TNIV).

Have you ever been there? Have you ever struck out? Burned bridges? Hit bottom? Have you ever been that alone? Alone is not a predicament; it's a place. Alone is a distant country, far from home where nobody cares and nothing is familiar to you. Alone is a prison cell, cold and abandoned, where the forgotten go to remember how things used to be. Once, they were frolicking. They threw caution to the wind. They lived far above their means. They footed the bill. But sooner or later, the party ended. The game was up. The rent came due, as it always does. Their buddies moved on. Only they were left. And no one gave them anything.

One night, in that place called *alone*, the prodigal had a conversion that changed his life.

"All of my father's servants have plenty of food," he said to himself, "but I am here, almost dying with hunger" (15:17 NCV). With that, the self-absorbed prodigal began a change of heart. He plotted a return to his father's farm, the same way he plotted his escape a few months earlier. Only now, he would go back as something else, something less.

"I will get up and go to my father," he said, "and I will say to him, 'Father, I have sinned against heaven and before you; I am no longer worthy to be called your son; treat me like one of your hired hands'" (15:18–19 NRSV).

But the father wouldn't hear it. While the prodigal was still a long way off in the distance, the father, who had been waiting on the porch every day for his son to return, ran out over the field to meet him. Kenneth Bailey writes about how uncommon it was for old men in that day to run: "An Oriental nobleman with flowing robes never runs anywhere," he says. "To do so is humiliating. . . . It is so very undignified in Eastern eyes for an elderly man to run. Aristotle says, 'Great men never run in public.'"[2] The father threw his arms around the boy, and the reunion began.

Very deliberately, the prodigal began to recite the lines he must have practiced all the way back to the farm. "Father, I have sinned against heaven and before you; I am no longer worthy to be called your son" (15:21 NRSV).

But the father hardly heard him. Before the prodigal could finish his line—the "treat me like one of your hired hands" part (15:19 NRSV)—the father ordered his slaves to bring out the family robe, fetch his signet ring, put sandals on the boy's feet, and kill the fattened calf. Then the father uttered words the prodigal could never have dreamed: "This son of mine was dead and is alive again; he was lost and is found!" (15:24 NRSV).

The beautiful story of the prodigal son is about forgiveness and second chances. But inside this is a plot even more beautiful. It is the story of a traveler, very far from home, who longs to come back as a slave and, instead, is granted every privilege of a child. It is about more than forgiveness. It is about, what Henri Nouwen calls, "a second-childhood." Nouwen writes,

"There is something in us humans that keeps us clinging to our sins and prevents us from letting God erase our past and offer us a completely new beginning. . . . While God wants to restore me to the full dignity of sonship, I keep insisting that I will settle for being a hired servant. But do I truly want to be restored to the full responsibility of the son? Do I want to be so totally forgiven that a completely new way of living becomes possible?"[3]

This new way of life—this restored status as the child of God—requires us to let go of who we've become, to become who we might have been. Nouwen continues, "Receiving forgiveness requires a total willingness to let God be God and do all the healing, restoring, and renewing. As long as I want to do even a part of that myself, I end up with partial solutions, such as becoming a hired servant. As a hired servant, I can still keep my distance, still revolt, reject, strike, run away, or complain about my pay. As the beloved son, I have to claim my full dignity and begin preparing myself to become the father."[4]

When we shift from Slave to Child, a very different perspective on God begins to emerge in our hearts. Fear is eclipsed by intimacy. We learn not only to obey God, but also to love him. We no longer hide from God; we confide in him. He is not merely a judge with a law to be obeyed; he is a father with a heart and a way to be imitated.

Dennis Kinlaw writes, "The relationship of every child to every parent is a reflection of the relationship between the first and the second persons of the Holy Trinity."[5] Indeed, every family on earth is a replica—some good, others bad—of the kind of relationship our Father wants to have with us. Other models are beneath his dream, less than the best. He wants us to be his children, not his slaves. Even when you ask to be his slave, he invites you, like the prodigal, to return as his child.

Do you know who you really are? Do you, as Paul put it, "understand the confident hope he has given to those he called" (Eph. 1:18 NLT)? You are a child of God, but you often live like a slave. Particularly if you grew up in the church, your identity as a child of God can become distorted into a duty, a kind of a routine service, a liturgical slavery. But remarkably, because of Jesus, you can pray to God as Father. He is *Abba* (Daddy) to you now.

One time, my dad wanted to congratulate me on something I (Dave) accomplished in the sixth grade. He took me to K-Mart and made a wide sweeping gesture with his hand toward the whole store from the entrance. He said, "To congratulate you, I'll buy you anything in this whole store tonight." My eyes widened as I thought of the possibilities.

At the time, I didn't have a full grasp on how money worked or how much money Dad had. So I sort of limited things in my mind. I didn't even look at the huge stereo systems, expensive bikes, or anything that cost more than one hundred dollars. Instead, I chose a cassette tape case that was less than fifty dollars. I was content with just that case. It was more than I could afford myself, for sure, so I chose that one. It was nice. Only many years later did I find out from Dad that he had one thousand dollars cash in his pocket that night. What's more, he brought his checkbook just in case that wasn't enough. In my selection, I limited his blessing in my life.

Imagine how much God has in his pocket for you. You don't ask God for all the spiritual power you could because you forget that you are his child. Like me and my earthly father, you don't realize all he could do for you, in you, and through you. Our Father in heaven has the "cattle on a thousand hills" (Ps. 50:10). A very wealthy man in the time of Christ might own the cattle on one or perhaps two hills. Jesus was saying that God has more for us than we can dream of. He has "immeasurably more than all we ask or imagine" (Eph. 3:20). He can do anything in you spiritually. God is limitless, but you limit what he does when you act as only his slave.

Slaves wonder where they stand with God. They lack confidence. They are consumed with laws, sin, judgment, and merely serving God. Children think of freedom, privileges, identity, and pleasing God.

Beth was turning sweet sixteen at the end of the month. She couldn't wait because she was sure she would ace the driver's test. Her dad said she needed to get straight As in order to be able to drive their car, but that shouldn't be a problem. She had been an A student all her life.

Beth was the good girl of the family. She never got in trouble. So this last week when she skipped a day of school it was a big deal.

Monday of that week was one of those terrible, horrible, no-good, very-bad days. All the little things were going wrong. She somehow overslept and missed the bus and didn't realize her sweater was on inside-out until the second period of school. By lunchtime, Beth was ready to head home. Then her boyfriend had the nerve to break up with her right there in the cafeteria. By the time she got home, she was a mess. She talked all evening with her mother about it—well, she mostly just cried—and her mother listened.

On Tuesday morning, Beth woke up with a big headache from too much crying the night before. To her surprise, her mother was in the kitchen sipping coffee in her pajamas. She was usually off to work by that time. She set down her cup, "So, honey, how's it looking today?"

She slumped into the kitchen chair: "I don't want to face him today—or anybody really." Beth was about to tear up again. That made her mad at herself.

"Then don't go."

Beth looked at her funny. "Did she just say I should skip school?" she wondered.

She rolled her eyes, telling her mother, "I can't do that."

"Why not?"

Beth said, "But, I have perfect attendance this year."

Her mom smirked: "How about I make you one of those cheap certificates you get for that on our home computer, then?"

"But, I don't want everyone to think it's all gotten to me."

"Why?" her mother asked.

"I'll look stupid."

Her mother didn't think they would and told her so. She also said that what they all think doesn't matter in the end anyway. She told Beth that she was her beautiful, intelligent, and loving daughter. And she added that she was a child of God most of all. That's who she was, and what her ex-boyfriend or everyone at school thought didn't matter in the slightest.

Her mom called into work and took a personal day. She even called the school and said that Beth was going to spend the day with her and wouldn't be coming in. Beth felt like she was getting away with something but went along with it.

They watched movies and played games and stayed in their pajamas until two in the afternoon. It was the best day of the year.

Beth was learning that she was much more than a slave; she was a child. Perhaps her mother was learning the same thing. No matter our age, we are children of God as Christians. We just need to act like it, and sometimes that means hanging out with our families in our pajamas instead of doing what everyone else wants us to do.

When we last left him, Jeff was just beginning to figure out his true identity. The greatest treasure stolen by the robbers in the middle of that night was not any loot they carried away from the house. It was the golden memories they bashed from his head. Many of those memories never returned. He still doesn't remember much of his past life. You might think this story doesn't have a happy ending, but it does.

His wife, family, friends, and church all told him who he was, and he rediscovered it for himself too. He learned about his family and how to be a son and brother all over again. He found out he had a wife, and he fell in love with her again. He met old friends who became new ones to him. He went back to his church for the first time with fresh eyes.

He was a Christian before, but he accepted Christ again. In a stunning example of what it means to be called by God, Jeff found out what his old job had been: youth pastor. After a leave of absence, he went back to the ministry. He reconfirmed his calling and went to Wesley Seminary at Indiana Wesleyan University to learn what it means to minister all over again. Just a few weeks ago, he shared his story on video for the people at College Church, and we were stunned to hear how God had taken his life and given it a new purpose, using him to minister to many through this experience.

Jeff's story doesn't have a bad ending; it's the happiest ending possible, and one that's still playing out by the grace of God. Those robbers stole his past, but God is restoring his wonderful future. And it all started with listening to what his true identity was.

God can do the same for you because you're his child, even if you have been acting like you're just his slave. You're so much more. You've just forgotten who you are—his child.

REFLECT AND WRITE

In what ways has God already made shifts in your soul from Slave to Child? Write your story and testimony of what God has done in you.

How might God be calling you to shift from Slave to Child in the coming year? Write how God has led you or what impressions you have received during this chapter.

SLAVE TO CHILD QUESTIONS

SOULSHIFT QUESTIONS YOU ASK YOURSELF

When you think about or pray to God, do you ever imagine what he would look like? Describe him. Is he friendly or fearsome?

Where or how did you learn to describe God this way?

What does it mean to be God's child? Which people are the children of God? What responsibilities and privileges come to your mind?

SOULSHIFT QUESTIONS YOU WILL NEED TO BE ASKED

If God is your Father, how does that change your relationships with other people?

Think back over the last month. What were the signs that God loves you?

What have you done this week that comes from being a slave? What have you done that comes from being a child?

SOULSHIFT QUESTIONS YOU WOULD DISCUSS WITH OTHERS

When someone gets involved with our ministry or group, are they more likely to feel like a child of God or like his slave?

How might seeing God as a loving Father change the way our church plans its ministry goals? What should we add or subtract if God is really a Father?

What is one thing that our group did this year that made it easier for people to see and accept God's love?

SEEN TO UNSEEN

**a shift in values from embracing things that
are temporary to embracing things that are eternal**

Because you have seen me, you have believed; blessed are those who have not seen and yet have believed" (John 20:29).

One time, during preparation for preaching on this passage, I (Dave) developed a list of my own observations from books I had read on doubt and on this chapter in the Bible. However, I couldn't get away from the hunch that someone I knew might have more to say about it than I did. So, I called a college student named Sarah who attends our church.[1]

Sarah told me that she's thought a lot about that verse. She talked about how we use the word *see* a little loosely sometimes. Even she does this, saying "I see what you're saying" or even "It's good to see you" when she doesn't really see you at all. You see (there, I did it again), Sarah is blind. She told me about the unique trust required when you are not able to see. She has to trust when others give directions that taking the second left, for example, will not put her at the top of a steep staircase that she could tumble down. She has to trust. Perhaps, she says, being one who doesn't see makes her more apt to trust God and to have faith in God's presence.

Sarah has always had a hard time when people in worship services say, "Picture Jesus' face right now and just worship him." She feels completely lost in these moments. She joked, "You know, Dave, I really have no idea what a Jewish man in the first century might have looked like." I confessed to her that such moments in services are deeply distracting to me, as I have this false image from art in my mind of a blue-eyed, blond-haired, European-looking Jesus. Perhaps, in some way, it's more limiting in that regard for me to have seen; I define Jesus too narrowly.

Sarah told me she believes that if she remains sightless her entire life, the very first thing she'll ever see is the face of Jesus Christ when her sight is restored in the next life. And that vision of Christ will be untainted. She doesn't have to filter through a thousand incorrect guesses at the face of Christ. The first thing she sees will be the most accurate and authentic thing she could ever see for she has believed without seeing her whole life. Perhaps those who have believed without seeing are blessed after all.

Regarding this interchange between Jesus Christ and doubting Thomas in John 20, N. T. Wright claims that "this isn't, then, so much a rebuke to Thomas; it's more of an encouragement to those who come later, to people of subsequent generations." Wright explains, "We are all 'blessed' when, without having seen the risen Lord for ourselves, we nevertheless believe in him."[2]

We have our doubts, to be sure. But as John Ortberg put it, "I must have truth. Therefore I doubt. . . . I must have hope. Therefore I believe."[3]

❧

For some, faith is a grand leap in the dark. It begins where reason ends. It is wishful thinking, recognized by a conspicuous lack of evidence. Whenever something doesn't make sense or seems too far out we say, "Have a little faith." Because of this, people of faith are often thought to be out of touch and less aware of the stark reality that is in front of them, reality that is plain for everyone to see. People of faith believe in God, though he cannot be seen. They believe in heaven, though they have never been there. And they believe in prayer, even though they cannot prove that it changes anything.

As the novelist Thornton Wilder put it, "[Faith] is nothing if it is not courageous; . . . if it is not ridiculous."[4] The Bible has a lot to say about such faith. It is the core of the Christian witness. Those who have it are said to be spiritually mature. But what, exactly, is it?

Perhaps faith is the capacity to see what is already there. Take Elisha, for example. He once found himself the subject of a very intense manhunt by the king of Aram who had it in for him (2 Kings 6:8–23). One night, while Elisha and his servant were sound asleep, the king of Aram discovered their whereabouts and hustled together a posse: "he sent horses and chariots and a strong force" to go after him (6:14). By the time morning came, the king's men were all in place. They had completely surrounded the city. As the sun was rising, Elisha's servant rose and went out for an early walk. The air was chilly. The sun was chasing away the fog of the last night. The servant felt alive. Then, all at once, he saw them! They were up in the hills, hundreds of them, and lining every road out of town. They were armed to the hilt, mounted on horses, and awaiting their command.

The servant panicked and ran back to Elisha. By the time he got there, he was out of breath. "What are we going to do?" he said. "The king's soldiers are crawling all over. They have surrounded the entire city, and there is no way out."

Remarkably, Elisha was not panicked at all. He calmly told the servant to not be afraid because "those who are with us are more than those who are with them" (6:16).

But what on earth could he mean? Didn't he know what was happening? The servant was sure that Elisha had not grasped the seriousness of the moment. Or perhaps he had already calculated some way of escape. Maybe he was just living in denial. Still, they had no way out, and as soon as he saw the army, the servant was sure that Elisha would understand the danger.

Fear is our natural response whenever we see something like the servant saw. It is the result of being hemmed in—without options, without escape, and without hope. Fear looks to the hills and counts the enemy. It calculates the chances for survival. It measures the resources within us against the enemy outside us, and if our resources are not enough, fear sends up a flag. We hear threats around us: The doctor breaks the news that we have cancer; the company warns of huge cutbacks; the project runs out of money; the plaintiff has the best lawyer in town. These things can rattle us, but they do not destroy us—at least not until we have run out of options.

But the moment it appears that we are hemmed in with no escape, like the servant seeing the enemy army, we are afraid. Sometimes we try to convince ourselves that the enemy is not really there, that perhaps we need to be more positive, but every morning we awake to the same old threat. We are still surrounded. The last efforts have failed. We have no way out.

Right then, Elisha prayed the most peculiar thing: "O LORD, open his eyes so he may see" (6:17). Strangely enough, Elisha was more worried about his servant than about the enemies he saw. He thought that the real problem was not what the servant had seen, but what the servant had not seen.

So he prayed a very different prayer. He prayed, not for protection or for escape, but instead for a miracle of vision. He wanted his servant to see something else, something more than what he had already seen. As he prayed, the Lord opened the servant's eyes, and this time, when he looked to the hills, he saw not only the enemy king's posse but also an army of God encompassed by fire and ready for battle. Who were they? Where did they come from? The servant turned to ask Elisha, and then noticed that Elisha himself was surrounded by chariots of fire.

No wonder the good prophet was so calm and collected. On that morning outside the city of Dothan, there were two realities, not one, and Elisha saw them both. He saw what the servant saw, that the hills were alive with his enemies. But he saw something else too. He saw another army that was already there, invisible to the servant, known but to God and himself. Elisha saw more than the servant. He saw both worlds.

Faith's work is not to ignore the stark reality of our enemies lying in wait surrounding us. Rather, faith's work is to remind us of another reality even greater than that of the enemy. Faith sees that our enemies have surrounded us. But it also sees that our God has surrounded our enemies, that "those who are with us are more than those who are with them" (6:16).

Faith does not speak things into existence. It simply sees what is already in existence, though still unseen to those who live by sight alone. Faith sees a world that runs alongside this world, and it lives according to what it sees in both worlds. Faith sees through the eyes of the soul. It sees now what everyone else will acknowledge later. Only faith sees it now.

Real faith sees that the economy tanked or that the tests came back positive or that the company is laying people off. But faith sees other things too. It sees that God can be trusted, the poor own the kingdom, the hungry may be full of the Spirit, those who mourn are loved, and those persecuted for righteousness' sake are treated like rock stars in the alternate reality that is the kingdom of heaven. Faith sees this now. It imagines a world where race, intellect, or money cannot divide us, where love is unselfish and sin is powerless. Faith sees the unseen, but the unseen is no less real just because it requires faith to see it.

Like God himself, people of faith call things that are not as though they were (Rom. 4:17). Then, sure enough, they are!

❦

It is the beginning of wisdom to doubt your doubt. Yann Martel writes about this in the beloved novel *Life of Pi*. "Doubt is useful for a while," young Pi, the narrator, tells us. "We must all pass through the garden of Gethsemane. . . . If Christ spent an anguished night in prayer, if He burst out from the Cross, 'My God, My God, why have you forsaken me?' then surely we are also permitted doubt. But we must move on. To choose doubt as a philosophy of life is akin to choosing immobility as a means of transportation."[5]

So, move beyond doubt, the philosophy of life where all that can be trusted is that which is seen. Thomas Merton reminded us that those who live only by what they can see live a life of despair. In his book *Life and Holiness*, Merton says the first step to this life of faith is not to reject reason but choose between two faiths: "One, a human, limited, external faith in human society," and the other a "faith in what we do not 'see,' . . . a faith that goes beyond all proofs, a faith that demands an interior revolution of one's whole self and a reorientation of one's existence."[6] In the shift from Seen to Unseen, one chooses this second faith.

Here's a way to think about what moving from Seen to Unseen feels like. Right now, put your right hand over your right eye. If your left eye is healthy, you can still see. Holding your hand over one eye does not prevent you from seeing. However, using only one eye, it's harder to tell how far away things are. You'll notice this most if you look into the distance. Now take your left hand and hold it up at arm's length in front of you, and then slowly move it to the right. You lose sight of it fairly quickly, don't you?

Having two eyes serves two purposes. First, the second eye brings dimension to the things the first eye sees, helping with depth perception and adding context and distance. The second eye also adds to your peripheral vision things that would be otherwise invisible to you—invisible not because they do not exist but because we are not using the second eye to see them.

Those who shift from Seen to Unseen have developed this second eye to see the kingdom of God.

Where are you? In a coffee shop? Your bedroom? Your office? Look around at the room in which you're sitting right now. Imagine that you poked a hole in the wall over there. What if you drilled a hole through that wall so you could see through it? And what if you saw an identically outfitted room on the other side of that wall? Same furniture. Same décor. Same layout. Same people. In that other room is another world, running parallel to yours — but many things there affect things, or even control things, in your world.

When you hear Jesus Christ speak in the Bible about the kingdom of God, you get the sense that there is this other world all around us, right next door, and most people don't see it, can't see it. However, this kingdom next door can be seen by you. You can drill through the barrier, even live in both worlds. You could change every conversation you are having in this room so that it aligns with the ones in the other room, the kingdom room.

No matter how old or young you are, you can have access to this kingdom. Don't think you have to be smarter to do so. In fact, Slave to Child reminds us that Jesus asks us to become like children to see it. It takes a childlike faith to shift from Seen to Unseen.

❦

Our culture tends to treat those who only believe in what they see as the smartest. Those who have the least faith in the unseen, only having faith in what can be touched, are esteemed as the most intelligent.

John Ortberg tells this story about the world's smartest man:

Three men are in a plane: a pilot, a Boy Scout, and also the world's smartest man. The engine fails, the plane is going down, and there are only two parachutes. The smart man grabs it. "I'm sorry about this," he says, "but I'm the smartest man in the world; I have a responsibility to the planet," and he jumps out of the plane. The pilot turns to the Boy Scout and speaks of how he has lived a long, full life and how the Boy Scout has his whole life in front of him. He tells the Boy Scout to take the last parachute and live. "Relax, Captain," the Boy Scout says. "The world's smartest man just jumped out of the plane with my backpack."[7]

Sooner or later, we all have to make the leap of faith, and sometimes smarts aren't enough. There are plenty of smart and not-so-smart people who have no faith in the unseen. And, of course, there are plenty of not-so-smart and very smart people who have just as much faith in the other world as the ground beneath their feet. Even a scientist can choose the parachute of faith in the unseen kingdom of God.

Take Connie, for example. She's a missionary in Central America. The things she's seen there in ten years of mission service are mind-bending. She loves working to help people. She wouldn't be there if she didn't. Restoring sight, helping people to get up and walk again—and they do it all through basic medical treatments that are common in the States. It's almost as though she gets to do miracles like Jesus did. Connie thought of herself as mostly a scientist during her years of training. Of course, the things she does aren't really miracles; she knows that. It's science. And she still loves the science. In fact, she wrote a handbook about the flora and fauna of the region where she works.

In her work there, however, there seems to be much more than meets the eye. Theologically, she's always believed that to be true. But the reality in her work is shocking. At times, there is a spirit of evil around certain people and places, she says. You just can't get past it. The people there are very superstitious. At first, she thought they were just primitive, but over time, she's grown to realize that they're afraid—and for good reason. You can sense the Enemy. She knows that sounds like crazy talk for a scientist like her, but she says, "I guess you just have to be here."

More than once, she's done all she could for a patient, and medically, she knew they were done for. In those times, she, the nurses, and assistants would lay hands on the person and pray for him or her. Then the preaching missionary would come in and anoint the patient with oil.

Usually, they died. But sometimes, they lived. Though it is rare, sometimes she sees it. She sees a glimpse of that other world and some miraculous things happen. She has X-rays to prove it. You might call her crazy, but ten years there has made her a better and more resourceful doctor. Even more, she's become more spiritually minded as a prayer warrior. There's more than meets the eye in this journey of life. We think we're all alone in this world, but God is there, right next to us all the time.

When my son was just eight years old, we went hiking in the woods. We hiked way out to the edge of the forest. I (Dave) said, "Max, do you think you could find your way back from here to the place we parked the car?" I reassured him, "I'll go with you, but I'll follow you. I won't tell you where to go—I'll just go wherever you go. You can do it, I'm sure."

So he started off. We got even more lost at first. He had me hiking over hills I hadn't seen before and through barbed wire fences and thorn bushes. It was crazy. But I showed my faith in him. I kept following. He changed his general direction a few times. But over time, I realized that he was basically getting us back the right way. Every time he doubted he could find his way, I said, "You're doing great buddy, just keep going. You'll make it."

And then I could sense that we were getting really close. I knew it before he did. All of a sudden, he stopped cold. He caught a glimpse of our car over the ridge. He looked over at me with a twinkle in his eye, and I've never been as proud as a father, and he's never been as confident as a son. High fives and hugs followed. I just knew he could do it.

Perhaps your heavenly Father has been there all along. You don't see him but he's following you, sure you can find your way back. If you pause, you might just notice that he's there, believing in you even when you doubt your belief in him. When you feel utterly lost, he keeps plodding there with you, through the thorns and over the hard hills. As you get closer to finding your way home, his heart swells with pride for you.

When you nearly lost faith in him, he never lost faith in you.

REFLECT AND WRITE

In what ways has God already made shifts in your soul from Seen to Unseen? Write your story and testimony of what God has done in you.

How might God be calling you to shift from Seen to Unseen in the coming year? Write what leadings God is giving you or the impressions you received during this chapter.

SEEN TO UNSEEN QUESTIONS

SOULSHiFT QUESTIONS YOU ASK YOURSELF

How often in a day do you look for God's activity?

What barriers keep you from seeing the unseen?

What is one thing in your life that currently requires faith?

SOULSHiFT QUESTIONS YOU WILL NEED TO BE ASKED

Who in your life encourages you to think about and talk about God's invisible presence and work?

Can you think of a time when you saw the presence or the activity of God in places where you did not expect to see it? What did it look like, and how did you know it was him?

Think of a time when God did not answer your prayers in the way you had hoped. How did you respond and why?

SOULSHiFT QUESTIONS YOU WOULD DISCUSS WITH OTHERS

Take an opportunity for people in the group to share where and how they have seen God at work.

Read Matthew 5–7 (the Sermon on the Mount), and consider it a description of that invisible world on the other side of the wall. What do you think are the greatest differences between that world and this one?

What can our group do differently to incorporate some of those differences from the unseen world?

4

CONSUMER TO STEWARD

**a shift in ownership from acquiring things for ourselves
to offering what we have to God and others**

Joey Chestnut had a dream. He didn't dream of hitting home runs or walking on the moon. He didn't plan to be a doctor or lawyer. Mr. Chestnut, at the prime age of twenty-six, longed to eat more than fifty hot dogs.

You might think Joey set his sights a bit low. Maybe you have eaten fifty hot dogs in your lifetime or maybe in a year. But Joey Chestnut dreamed of eating those fifty hot dogs in one sitting, in less than twelve minutes, in world-record time.

Nathan's Famous Hot Dog Eating Contest occurs every year on the Fourth of July on Coney Island. Since 1916, this Super Bowl of swallowing is where the best competitive eaters go to gorge down buckets of dogs to the cheers of adoring, and usually grossed-out, fans of the International Federation of Competitive Eating (IFOCE).

In 2006, Joey Chestnut was the underdog of hot dog gurgitation. The undisputed king of eating was Joey's nemesis, Takeru Kobayashi. Dubbed "The Tsunami," Kobayashi was in the midst of an unbeatable streak. He inaugurated his dominance in 2001, his first year of competition. The ironically slim, one-hundred-twenty-pound Takeru stunned the crowd by inhaling the first twenty-five (the previous record), then going on to double it at fifty. The judges ran out of markers and had to begin handwriting the number of each hot dog that went down his tiny gullet. The small Japanese Tsunami left a wake of unsuspecting huge men groaning in pain as they tried to keep up.

Since then, no one had touched the Takeru Tsunami in competition. He was a weapon of mass digestion.[1] But Joey Chestnut had his dream. He entered "training" by fasting and by stretching his stomach with milk, water, and protein supplements, downing gallons quickly to enhance the competitive elasticity of his innards. In 2006, the training paid off as Joey Chestnut did what no man or woman had been able to do in half a decade: out-eat Takeru Kobayashi.

In just the first few minutes of the lightning-fast competition, Chestnut outpaced the Tsunami, beating him to ten, then twenty, then thirty HDBs (the official IFOCE unit of eating one hot dog in a bun).[2] The Tsunami seemed destined to finally fail. Red-faced and sweating like marathon sprinters, the two men chased hot dog inhaling glory. In the waning seconds, with just over one hot dog separating them, Joey Chestnut broke the world record and achieved his dream, having shoved fifty-two dogs down without any of them coming back up.

The only problem is that the Tsunami had surpassed his own record as well, eating fifty-three, and adding another three-quarters of a dog for good measure, establishing the new record at 53.75 HDBs. Looking as if he was about to expire or explode (or both), Chestnut said to the reporters: "I'm heartbroken a little bit . . . I got a little bit tired. I should have pushed harder."[3]

Recommitted to competitive eating after this defeat, Chestnut didn't let his dream die. He came back in 2007, and defeated Takeru for the first time.

Even though the Tsunami ate sixty-three hot dogs this time, Chestnut reached sixty-six and has held the title each year since.[4] But don't feel bad for the Tsunami. He still holds the records for eating the most Johnsonville brats, rice balls, and lobster rolls. He also still holds the record for the most cow brains eaten—almost eighteen pounds in just fifteen minutes—a record no one is particularly interested in taking from him.

It seems fitting that our world has made the act of eating into a spectator sport. We've become world-class consumers, and anyone can get in the game. Like the hot dog eating contest, our lives have become about volume and speed. How much can we get how fast?

Sixty years ago, Americans ate 144 pounds of meat and poultry per person. Now, we consume over 220 pounds per person.[5] While Americans comprise only 7 percent of the world's population, we consume a disproportionate amount of the world's oil, water, money, cars, and just about everything else. In fact, each year, we spend more money on advertising than most countries spend on everything, and much of what we spend "is used to convince us that Jesus was wrong about the abundance of possessions."[6] The wealthiest 20 percent of the world now accounts for over 75 percent of total private consumption. The poorest 20 percent account for less than 2 percent of private consumption.

We hyper-consume by buying products labeled *green* or *organic* as well. Marketers and corporations have caught on to this trend and have channeled it into even more consumption. Now, we feel less guilty buying a 50 percent larger flat-screen TV when it's marketed as 50 percent more energy efficient. God bless us for saving the planet!

Our consumer mentality stretches to nearly every facet of our lives. It's not limited to cheeseburgers and sodas. It moves beyond clothing, jewelry, and perfume. Our politics is rife with consumer mentality. Candidates have moved from diplomats into brands. Even our music and art is determined more by what sells than by something that rests in the artist's own soul. Our work has become a way to pay the bills. As the professional athlete Rasheed Wallace put it, "I don't give [expletive] about no trade rumors. As long as somebody CTC [cuts the check] at the end of the day, I'm with them . . . I just go out there and play. So long as somebody CTC."[7]

Education and health care, once the realm of mentors and selfless heroes, is now marketed like everything else. Billboards tout the skills of this or that hospital's heart surgeons like they are star ball players intended to fill the seats of an arena. During the nightly news, the commercials are just as likely to sell medications for your depression as they are to sell automobiles. And have you been in a Christian bookstore lately? Yes, the spiritual domain has its own problems with consumerism. Skye Jethani walks us through this phenomenon in his penetrating book *The Divine Commodity*. He points out that we've turned God and Christianity into a consumable product, and that we must deal with this before growing spiritually. Jethani wonders if "the contemporary church has been so captivated by the images and methods of the consumer culture that it has forfeited its sacred vocation to be a countercultural agent of God's kingdom in the world?"[8]

As we've seen from numerous surveys and studies, sociologists can't seem to find a difference in the lives of Christians and non-Christians anymore. No matter where you live, you have probably contracted some form of cultural virus. It isn't your fault. If you live in the United States of America, you happen to live in a country that boasts the wealthiest culture in the history of the world. You don't have to apologize for where you were born. But do have the good sense to ask yourself if any of the culture is rubbing off on you? Ask yourself these questions:

- Do I see other people's stuff and become critical or bored with my own?
- Do I shop for recreation?
- Do I buy compulsively (because I feel like it) without thinking first of my budget or of my need?
- Is my circle of need getting bigger (such as, cell phones, iPods, larger homes)?
- Do I complain a lot about how much I make (such as, my salary or tips)?
- Do I feel self-conscious when I am around rich people?

- Do I give less than 10 percent of my income to the ministry of the church?
- Does it annoy me when the preacher talks about money?

Jethani says that Christians today think and behave in ways that are more similar to those of the world. And why? Because "we have abandoned the vision that Christianity is an alternative way."[9]

⤝

What is this alternative way? It begins with a suspicion that Jesus was right about possessions after all. He talked about them constantly. Howard Dayton has actually counted the times: "Sixteen of the [thirty-eight] parables were concerned with how to handle money and possessions. Indeed, Jesus Christ said more about money than about almost any other subject. The Bible offers [five hundred] verses on prayer, fewer than [five hundred] verses on faith, but more than 2,350 verses on money and possessions."[10]

Yes, Jesus had strong opinions about money, but he had more than just opinions. He had an entirely different mind. To him, money was not a symbol. It was a lever to get something done. It had no inherent value apart from the opportunities it could create. For the moment, put yourself inside one of his parables (Matt. 25:14–30) and you will see what we mean. You will journey from being Consumer to Steward.

Let's say you're the servant to a very wealthy landowner. One day, your master decides to take the year off and travel the world. He calls you into the mansion, together with two of your friends, and divides up his property between the three of you. He says that he has divided his property into shares, or talents, and that he has arranged for each of you to get a certain amount. To one, he will give five shares; to another, two; and then he turns to you and gives you one.

It is the nature of consumers to compare. They are always wanting, counting, and measuring their salaries and protecting their assets. They are always worried about their number. So you start to wonder why you got cheated out of more shares. Have you done something wrong? Does your master love you as much as the others? Haven't you been just as faithful to him as they were? And don't you deserve it for all your hard work? Why the difference?

It turns out that this is the first lesson on your way to stewardship: Possessions are not earned; they are given. Every steward knows this. As long as you think possessions are earned, you will compare yours with others—with what you could have had or with what you were expecting to have—and you will always be disappointed.[11] Once you learn that even possessions you work for are given to you, you are free from their tyranny. You don't have to protect them, serve them, measure them, or feel deprived for not having them. Now you can use them instead of consume them.

So, the master sends you on your way, each with your own talents, your own shares of the estate. When the year is over, he summons you back to the mansion to give an account. Of course, your five-talent friend can hardly wait. He's done quite well. He says, "Master, you entrusted me with five shares, and look here, I have gained five more."

You can't believe what you're hearing. How did he do that? It must be easier when you have more to work with. That's what you tell yourself and you half believe it until your other friend speaks up. "Master," he says, "you entrusted me with two shares, and look here, I have gained two more." Uh oh. This blows up your alibi. Until now, you were sure that some people have it easier than you, and that's why they're so generous, frugal, or wise with their possessions. But here, right before your eyes, is a two-talent man who is just as faithful as the five-talent man. Go figure! And while your head is still spinning, the master speaks.

"Well done," he says. "You have been faithful with a few things so I will put you in charge over many things." You can't believe what you're hearing. It turns out that stewardship is not about what you have but about how you use it. It's a state of mind. Stewards are always asking, "How can I leverage what I have into something more for God?" But consumers are always asking, "How can I protect what I have so that I don't lose it for myself?" The real difference between you and your friends is not what's in your wallet, but what's in your heart.

Then the master turns to you. And before he can say a word, you start looking down at your shoes. "Ummm . . . Master." You can hardly get it out. You were going to say that you had nothing to work with until the two-talent guy blew your cover. So you decide to blame it now on the master himself. "He is a hard man," you say under your breath. "He harvests where he did not sow and gathers where he did not scatter." But your master is waiting for your report. You open your mouth, but the words are frozen in your throat.

Finally they come: "I was afraid." It sounds terrible, but you might as well say it. "I was afraid . . . and so I went out and buried your talent in the ground." The words land with a thud. The master has graciously given you his property. He has invested a part of himself with you. He has entrusted you with a piece of his own future. And you buried it. You were afraid.

As you stand there, holding that one talent, you notice yet another stark difference between yourself and the stewards: Stewards have a fundamentally different vision of the master. To them, the master is generous. He believes in his servants, so he entrusts them with his possessions. He is easy to please. However, to consumers, the master is stingy. He is partial to the rich and hard on the poor. And so he is impossible to please.

"Come," says the master, as he gestures the stewards toward his side. "Come and share in my happiness." As you wonder what will happen to you next, your first surprise is what just happened to them. Consumers are accustomed to thinking of reward as more talents, as a greater share of the whole. But the master's chief interest is for the steward's happiness. The steward's most-coveted thing is never the master's possessions but the master's happiness.

So while the master is passing his happiness to the stewards, you turn to face your consequences. Perhaps they will not be as bad as you fear. Or perhaps he will give you another go at it. "If only he would give me another chance," you say to yourself. "The next time I will get it right."

~≈

So how can we begin to practice this shift from Consumer to Steward? It will look different for each person, but in every steward's life, there are three components, each of which is a mini-shift marking another step in the journey.

The first mini-shift is from being spenders to being savers. Call it contentment. This is a shift from, "When I get that, I'll be happy" to "This is enough!" In this shift, we recognize that if we are not already content with what we have, we will never be content with what we want, for contentment is a learned behavior. We must learn to stop eyeing the next bargain, stop using debt to keep up with the wealthy, stop growing the number of things we "need" to live on, and stop sprawling into bigger homes and more luxurious cars. Live simply. Buy what you need and then stop buying. Use coupons. Eliminate waste. Spend time to save money. Fix it yourself. Use it longer. Recycle it. Carry less cash in your wallet, and don't use the credit card for items you can't pay off within the month. Remember, "what you can afford" does not mean the credit-limit on your charge cards or the monthly payment. What you can truly afford is determined by the way it plays off of other interests, other debts, and other values in your life. If you think like this, you will find that you sometimes cannot afford to buy what you easily have the money for. When you live contentedly, you lift up your fish and loaves—your meager existence—before a generous God and you say, "This is enough!" And when you do this, you will stop bleeding money out the sides of your life, so that you can direct it to places it was intended to go.

This doesn't mean that you buy nothing. It means that you use what you buy, that you keep on using it, and that you buy what it takes for you to produce in the way God has called you to produce.

~≈

The second mini-shift is from saver to giver. Call it sharing. Sociologists have long noticed a trend in American giving: the more we have, the less we give. This won't surprise most kids. They know that poor people often give away bigger candy bars at Halloween. When I (Steve) was a kid, my friends would hit the high-rent districts in town, while I would hang out in the poorer neighborhoods (where I fit in). I would come home with a pillow-case full of candy—big candy, expensive candy. On the day after Halloween, my bedroom was like aisle six at Wal-Mart. I would take it upstairs, count it, smell it, and run my fingers through it. I would stand back and appreciate it and imagine what it was going to taste like when I ate it.

Later, my parents would ask for a "tithe" from my candy. Can you believe it? They wanted a cut. They would always ask in the kindest of ways: "Say, would you have an extra Snickers bar up there in your room?" or "What are you going to do with those Butterfingers, since you don't like them?" Still, I took this rather hard. It was like I had to pay rent for living there. How could my parents have the nerve to ask for my petty little candy bars? Couldn't they just take one of those religious tracts some well-meaning Christians always dropped in my bag? No, they wanted more. They wanted something valuable. They wanted the same thing I wanted. Only I had it first.

Years later, when I had my own children, I learned why. It had nothing to do with the candy (well, almost nothing). My parents weren't trying to steal my stash. They were trying to break me of my stuff. They were trying to teach me to share. Yes, it paid a little to them, but I would be the real winner if I could learn to divest myself of something that was valuable to me.

It turns out that stinginess is not my problem alone. Many Christians these days really struggle with sharing anything they consider to be important. Like me, they are happy to share their Butterfingers but never their Snickers. This is nowhere more obvious than in the way Christians tithe. It is one of the first places where our souls need to shift. By referring to a tithe as a "charitable contribution," we have reserved for ourselves the option of not giving at all. Many Christians have misconceptions about the tithe: (1) that the word itself means "giving," rather than "tenth;" (2) that it is recommended but not commanded in Scripture; (3) that it can be given to any charitable organization, not only to the church; (4) that it comes off the bottom, not the top of our income; and (5) that it should go to whatever cause we most believe in.

Perhaps you're like many of us, and you're completely willing to address more general spiritual issues, but once money comes up you get uncomfortable and begin thinking like a consumer. If so, or if you're already gearing up right now to argue this point, we urge you to seek God's guidance on the shift from Consumer to Steward; this issue may be more important for you than you think.

The Bible urges that a "tenth of one's possessions" be given to one's place of worship. But actually, in the Bible there are four different ways to share. One is this tithe—a tenth of our income given out of obligation with a heart of thanksgiving to the place where God dwells; to the place where there is an altar (Mal. 3:8–12). Another is an offering—any amount given in addition to our tithe to a cause that God has laid on our hearts (1 Cor. 16:2; 2 Cor. 9:7). A third is an act of benevolence—a gift or an act of service to the poor done in a spirit of compassion with the intent of restoring their dignity (Luke 14:13; 1 Tim. 6:17–18). A fourth way to give is a bequest—an amount of money left behind by those who are dying for causes and places that matter the most to them (Prov. 13:22).

❧

Dan works at a waste management company—not just any waste management company but the biggest one in the state. A year ago, at the age of thirty-five, Dan was promoted to regional director. A nice new office, a big raise, a company car—he was finally getting some perks in life.

His family started doing a lot of things they hadn't done before. They started a college-saving fund, since they had a three-year-old and another one on the way. They also started putting away money to take a big ten-year-anniversary cruise—with all the extras. Everything was starting to look up.

The timing at church had been uncanny. Just as Dan started to make a bit more money, the minister launched into a sermon series on stewardship. The first sermon was all about the storehouse tithe. Dan had just spent that whole weekend searching the Internet for a Jet Ski, but over lunch that day, he and his wife had a serious discussion. After thinking and praying about it, they decided that, for the first time, they were going to trust God by giving a full 10 percent tithe and then another 5 percent for missions and relief work.

So Dan didn't get his Jet Ski. In some ways, he's living pretty much the same way he did before the raise a year ago. It's been hard for him and his wife to adjust from dropping twenty dollars into the offering plate every week to writing a big check every other week, but they're convinced that it is part of what God is asking them to do. They are learning that possessions are not earned, but given; that their possessions are not really theirs, but God's. They are starting to see that God is very generous, and they are beginning to experiment with different ways to give. Imagine what will happen in their lives when their souls have shifted to see all of their possessions (even the ones they keep) as expressions of their love for God.

A third mini-shift is from sharing to blessing. Call it generosity. People who are generous have shifted from Consumer to Steward. They see themselves as servants who manage what God has given, and they use their resources, position, status, and time to bless those whom God wants to bless. Consumers always want to be on the receiving end of this blessing. But stewards want to bless others.

Jeremiah and Jan are in their late sixties, and he retired this past summer. They have an RV now and head out wherever and whenever they want all year round. They're having the time of their lives. He tells people, "I think I was born to be retired."

But it's been a bit of a challenge in one unexpected way. This is the first time since Jeremiah was eighteen that he's actually making less money than the year before. Since they first started to intentionally give and tithe, he and Jan had given more every year. They had been incredibly blessed financially, and they gave, sacrificially at times, in order to advance the kingdom. They became accustomed to giving more and more. He would say, "It's a rush to see our money go to such good causes and do great things in the kingdom we could never do ourselves."

But this year, they have much less to give. They've already tithed on all the money they've made; and they're still giving something, even though they're not making any new income. It's just a habit for them to keep giving. They're trying to figure out what it means to steward their resources in the middle of this transition. They think about what kind of an inheritance they'll pass on. They worry about whether their church will have enough funds the next time they need to build, even if they are not around to see it.

This is new territory for Jeremiah and Jan. They're still learning what it will mean for them to be stewards in their aging years. Their biggest fear is that, now that they're older, they will just consume their way into the grave. They want to bless others, but they're worried that they don't have as much to offer now that they can't afford to give what they once did. But still, Jeremiah and Jan have made the shift from Consumer to Steward because generosity is not an amount, but a disposition in the heart.

✦

When our giving passes through the lens of grace, it becomes generosity. Grace expands both our hearts and the amount of our giving by making it the fruit of internal impulses rather than of external pressure. Generous people are usually simple in their giving. They do not quibble over the question of gross or net. They do not interrogate every cause that comes along. They do not give with strings attached or follow their money after they give it to make sure that the organization did everything they wanted them to do. Generous people see God as a giver, and they see themselves as his stewards. They often give before they can afford to give. They start when they still have very little and teach themselves to think first of others.

Generous people give before they are asked to give. They do not need clever gimmicks or slick brochures or somebody's free book as a way of saying thank you. And they do not limit their giving only to those who have asked or to the amount that they asked for. Generous people make a pact with God that they will be generous with their assets if only God will provide the opportunity. So they have already parted with their possessions even before they have given them away. Sometimes they even give to people or places that frustrate them simply because they believe that, in spite of their frustrations, God is blessing those people or that place.

As a result, generous people often become rich, so that they can be even more generous. God blesses what little seed they have given with an abundance of seed so that they, in turn, may reinvest their abundance into the work that God is doing.

Near the end of the movie *Schindler's List*, Oskar Schindler, who has already done so much, begins to weep and cry out over the lives he could have changed if he had only done more. He realizes that, if he had only sold his car, he could have saved ten Jews from death. Or by hocking the ring on his finger, he could have saved two Jews . . . or at least one Jew, he reasons—one person for the price of one ring. Even after all he'd done, he considered what more he could have done with his resources.

When you, as John Wesley said, earn all you can and save all you can in order to give all you can, you are showing that something has shifted far below the surface. Your soul is shifting from Consumer to Steward. This is true with more than just your money. It has to do with how you consume time, products, and relationships, and how disposable such things might be for you. It involves determining to steward them as though they are all on loan to you from God—because, of course, they are.

Consumers have a list of wishes. They are not content, and they obsess over salary, status, labels, and brands. Stewards use less and use it longer. They are not wasteful. They give more than they take, and they give more cheerfully.

Will you make a pact with God to become a better steward of your things? There is no point denying that consumerism has taken hold of our culture—of every culture. We might as well admit to the truth that we like stuff—that it is fun to buy and own. There is nothing to be gained by criticizing ourselves for having things that God has given us. Rather, God wants to use those things to train us in godliness. He wants us to use them to help accomplish his work around the world.

"In developing our skill at giving, we unify our entire self," said Wesley Willmer, "and [we] come into a more genuine relationship with God. By giving more of ourselves (time, money, talents), we are also giving more of ourselves to God, shaping our own souls."[12]

REFLECT AND WRITE

In what ways has God already made shifts in your soul from Consumer to Steward? Write your story and testimony of what God has done in you.

How might God be calling you to shift from Consumer to Steward in the coming year? Write what leadings God is giving you or impressions you received during this chapter.

CONSUMER TO STEWARD QUESTIONS

SOULSHIFT QUESTIONS YOU ASK YOURSELF

How does the fact that God is the giver of all good gifts influence you in your day-to-day living?

How easily do you share? Can you give examples?

Do you tithe regularly? Do you volunteer your time and talent at your church? Why or why not?

SOULSHIFT QUESTIONS YOU WILL NEED TO BE ASKED

Would those who know you call you generous or stingy? What symptoms do you have of either?

How content are you? Give examples of times when you were content or discontent.

When was the last time you felt prompted by the Holy Spirit to give something (time, talents, money), and what did you do in response to that prompting?

SOUL_{SH}iFT QUESTIONS YOU WOULD DISCUSS WITH OTHERS

What happens to our group when we discuss money? What is the collective "feel" of the group and why?

Are we a giving group? Share examples.

How do we help one another discover joy in generosity? How do we create opportunities for people to give?

ASK TO LISTEN

**a shift in posture from asking others
to listening to God**

One Tuesday afternoon, Sherri Collins was using sign language to communicate to her husband, "talking" as they normally do. For forty-two years, Sherri had not heard a word. But something was different this day. At first she wasn't sure what was different. But then she realized: she was *hearing* something.

Sherri had built a great life for herself. She attended public school until she was twelve. She graduated from the Illinois School for the Deaf, went on to college, and even got a master's degree. She got married and had a successful career, even becoming the executive director of the Arizona Commission for the Deaf. She had everything she might want—but one thing, of course, was still missing: hearing. Born profoundly deaf, she relied on reading lips and sign language to communicate.

On that Tuesday afternoon, however, all that started to change. For the first time, she heard something. Sherri suddenly stopped signing to her husband and turned to the audiologist assisting her. "Oh, I can hear him signing," she said to the woman. "His hands make noise. I didn't know that."[1]

She began to notice all the small nuances of hearing she had never experienced. She first noticed that her husband's hands made a noise when they smacked together to make a point while signing. Then all the other small sounds started to flow over her: the sound of an air conditioner humming, the sound of a pen scratching on paper, and the sound of the door opening behind her as someone entered the room. Asked what she was experiencing, Collins said, "It's overwhelming; I don't know how to explain it. It's way beyond what I expected."

Sherri Collins was hearing for the first time because her new cochlear implants had just been activated. These implants enable deaf people to interpret sounds in their brain in such a way that they "hear" much like hearing people. Those who have this procedure are still deaf, in a technical sense, even though they can hear in another way. One schoolteacher who has implants said, "Yes, I can hear, but I still consider myself deaf. . . . Now, I feel like I have the best of both worlds. I feel like I'm bilingual."

Sherri Collins had been anticipating many things after this procedure, wondering what it would be like to experience the hearing life. She looked forward to hearing a radio, which had so far been a useless instrument in her life. Music in particular was a fascination. But more than anything, she was looking forward to hearing a voice speaking "with clarity and nuance."

We long to hear a voice too. Even though most of us can physically hear, we are all spiritually deaf when we begin. It is difficult to know how to listen to the one voice we most want to hear: the voice of God.

It's hard to hear an inaudible voice. In fact, you might call it crazy. If someone says you're the kind of person who hears voices, it's not a compliment. They mean you hear voices that aren't really there. But that's where Christians beg to differ. We think God is really there. Referring to the voice of God, Max Lucado often says, "The One who spoke still speaks." The voice of God is more than past tense; it's present as well.

～

"I'm leaving!"

The words hung in the air.

The disciples were mumbling, almost to the last man, so maybe none of them even heard it at first. They were still collecting themselves. Jesus had just predicted Judas' betrayal, and as Jesus handed the treasurer his bread, all hell broke loose, literally (John 13:27). Even if you had seen this coming, even if you were the Son of God, you couldn't act like this didn't bother you. Somewhere in the commotion of Judas leaving and the disciples arguing—first over who would do such a thing and then over who would never do such a thing—Jesus' words were lost (Luke 22:23–34).

So he said it again: "I will be with you only a little longer" (John 13:33).[2]

This time, no one said a word. They just looked at him—blank stares. A few nodded. It felt like the wheels were beginning to come off after three good years of walking on water and raising the dead. Every day, it seemed, there was another miracle or argument with the Pharisees. The disciples must have gotten used to it, and now all of it was ending in one night.

Then he moved on to another subject. "So you must love one another like I have loved you," he said. "After all, this is how everyone will know that you're my disciples" (13:34–35 paraphrase). He was smiling again. This was among his favorite subjects. Whenever he spoke about love, there was levity in his voice. He called it a command, but it was more an invitation, a description of a place they would love if they could only find it within them. But Peter was not in the mood for another lecture on love. He was still stuck on the part about Jesus leaving. So he interrupted him.

"Where are you going?" (13:36). Then Thomas said, "Lord, we don't know where you are going" (14:5). The disciples had misunderstood

Jesus—as usual. So he explained that they couldn't follow him (13:36), and that they wouldn't need to: "I will ask the Father, and he will give you another Counselor to be with you forever—the Spirit of truth" (14:16–17).

Now slow down and read the rest: "The world cannot accept him, because it neither sees him nor knows him. But you know him, for he lives with you and will be in you. . . . It is for your good that I am going away. Unless I go away, the Counselor will not come to you; but if I go, I will send him to you. . . . But when he . . . comes, he will guide you into all truth . . . taking from what is mine and making it known to you" (14:17; 16:7, 13–14).

Imagine the advantages of living in the time of Jesus. If you needed anything from God, you only had to find Jesus and ask him for it. Whatever Jesus said and did, even if it was a pause or inaction, was the will of God for you. But now all of that was going away, and the disciples would be left to themselves. Why didn't Jesus stick around? Why not live here forever, or at least until we all die? That way we'd know where we stand with God. We wouldn't have to wonder if we were really going to heaven. We could just ask. And we would know exactly what God wanted us to do. We wouldn't have to worry about our friends becoming Christians, we could just send them to Jesus—literally—and he could convince them himself. Why must he go away?

Do you know how many times I (Steve) have wondered that? I wonder when standing at the side of a man in the oncology ward of a hospital just after he has received the grim news that his cancer has spread all over his body. I wonder when helping a middle-aged woman sort through her emotions about her husband who has just abandoned her, taken all their belongings, and walked out without telling her where he was going. What is God's will for her? Should she file for divorce? I wonder when I talk to my friend who is extremely smart, but doesn't believe in God, though he respects everyone's right to believe what they want. All my arguments, my apologetics, and my philosophy, bounce off him like BBs off the Rock of Gibraltar. He wants proof. What do I say, God?

I have definitely wrestled with the same question the disciples had: "Why does Jesus have to go?" It seems everything would be easier if he stuck around.

It turns out that I am too much like the disciples and not enough like Christ. Jesus is sure that his leaving is a very good thing. He says it is for our good—"It's better for you that I leave" (16:7 MSG). At first, this might sound like backpedaling—like something you say after you break up with someone ("Well, it's probably for the best") or when someone gets terminated from his job ("It's what he needs; it will make him stronger"). We say these things to soften the blow, to be nice. But Jesus never says anything just to be nice. He actually means it. It is as if he is saying, "If you knew what I know, you wouldn't be sad about me leaving. No, you would be glad that the day has finally come."

The secret, he says, is learning to listen to another voice—one that is not just with you (as Jesus was), but one that is in you, too. He is asking you to make a transition in your faith from an external voice to an internal voice; from asking someone outside to asking the Spirit who is inside; from asking for advice to listening for an impulse; from being taught to being led; from obedience to discernment; and from Ask to Listen. You may be thinking, "Whoa, that's a lot to ask!" You're right—this is a pretty big shift.

Even after we have walked with God a while, we still tend to get our answers more from without than from within. Our problem is not that we seek the counsel of wise friends, follow good leaders, or trust informed voices. It is more that we seek only these things and never learn to hear the voice of God within us. We are afraid we will confuse it with our own voice, as if the two voices were always different. We ask, "What would Jesus do?" but the voice within is saying, "Why not get to the place where what you would do is the same thing Jesus would do?"

"The persons who have most influenced us," said Fred Craddock, are those who "carried in them a silence that was the context for their words and actions."[3] To my surprise, Jesus is not content with getting me to obey him. Rather, he wants his voice to resonate with mine. He wants me to think his thoughts after him. He is calling you out of the white noise of voices you're used to into a silence that is very strange but true. In that silence,

God speaks in you.

A few decades ago, Earl was just starting out in life. He had an OK job—but it wasn't one where he could get ahead very far. He and his wife wanted to have kids, but they only made enough to rent a two-bedroom place. They just weren't sure they were ready to make the leap. But Earl had an opportunity that could change all that.

One of his high school buddies owned a specialized auto parts place in Ohio. It had taken off a few years earlier because he had a great regional retail business and had supplied some larger companies nationwide. When he was able to expand to a new retail store, he offered Earl a top sales job, where he would get a base salary that was almost the same as his old salary, but with commission on top of that. Even in a bad year, he would make more than before. In a good year, it would be doubled. His friend offered a small percentage ownership deal, too, if he worked for him a year and wanted to buy in to fund future retail expansions. On top of all this, he really liked his buddy in Ohio and thought he would be great to partner with. Earl and his wife were leaning toward going.

Then they started floating the idea to other people to see what they thought. Their parents, pastor, friends, and coworkers—they all had different perspectives on the idea. They would be leaving their hometown. The schools might not be as good in Ohio. Some thought the salary shouldn't be a factor in the decision. Others thought it was the main factor. Some said to go because they'd always remain friends even at a distance. Others told them to stay because they thought the distance would be too great to remain friends. They just couldn't get a common opinion on the offer and so their process stalled for a few weeks, and Earl and his wife didn't know where to turn.

That's when Earl heard a sermon that gave him some insight. The preacher talked about the idea of a day alone with God. The concept fascinated him. So, Earl took the next Saturday, went to a state park, walked around in nature all morning, and spent the afternoon at a coffee shop, thinking, praying, and listening. It was an amazing experience for him. He was really resistant to the idea of taking a day off, but he found that it was more restoring to him physically, emotionally, and definitely spiritually than any day off he'd ever had. And what's more, he felt this huge sense of God's presence that day and was about 99 percent positive about what they should do.

Earl went home and told his wife that they should step out in faith and move to Ohio. He thought she would burst into tears because all the other advisors had really driven home the point to her that they shouldn't move. But instead, she said that in her morning devotions, she had the same leading. She was praying that God would say the same thing clearly to Earl if he really wanted them to move. So they set off, after listening to God's voice in their lives, and started over again in another place.

⫷

A spiritual shift happens in you when you go from Ask to Listen, when you shift from an external motivation to an internal one. This doesn't mean that we never listen to others or that we don't seek advice. Instead, it means that we learn to listen first to God and seek his voice before turning to others. This shift has much to do with prayer. You are likely prone to think of prayer as talking to God or asking from God. But learning to listen in prayer is what shifts the soul most surely to the Holy Spirit.

So far, I (Dave) don't have hearing problems, although playing my iPod too loud all these years might catch up to me. But I do have a relative with some significant hearing troubles. She's lost nearly all hearing in her right ear. One of the things I've noticed is that she'll turn her head a bit to make sure the sound of a voice is going in the correct ear. Since it's her right ear that doesn't pick up the sound, she makes sure she's sitting so that her left ear is toward the TV or that she's sitting in a certain spot around the dinner table so she can pick up on most of the conversation. She has to be far more intentional about her position in the room or around the table than she used to be. Even choosing a chair is all about listening intentionally.

In a similar way, we need to be intentional about our listening. In some areas of our lives, we've grown deaf to the voice of God. We've tuned him out or listened to other voices over his. We've positioned ourselves in ways where we can't hear him like we could. We've turned a deaf ear to our Lord.

But it's beautiful when you purposefully posture yourself toward God. You begin to walk into rooms thinking, "How might I get into a position in here where I can hear the voice I need to hear most—God's voice?" This is what the shift from Ask to Listen is all about.

At first you may ask what God wants you to do, always dependent upon someone, even God, to tell you the answer. You might consult books, preachers, and counselors. You might listen to talk radio, click to websites, post polls on Facebook, or even text your friends for advice. You ask everyone and everything that might immediately suggest what you should do next, what is right or wrong. You could even use the Bible like this, as a kind of road map to heaven or a desk reference for controversial questions.

But the more you make this shift from Ask to Listen, the more you will learn to live with the ambiguous and the more you will experience the quiet of life—the times to contemplate, the season of waiting. In this shift, you listen with your heart for the still, small voice of God instead of looking for it in the fire, thunder, or wind. It is in this still, small voice that you find simplicity; you discover he is speaking to you and you trust your ability to know it.

Before making this shift, we try to get God to speak our language, at our time, and on our agenda. Our language is the audible voice, which is the only voice we know how to hear at first. Our time is structured by our decisions and his will; we ask for his direction in timely choices. Our agenda is what we're asking God for; we want to hear from God about the subjects that are on our mind.

After moving from Ask to Listen, however, a Christian becomes bilingual, much like the person mentioned earlier with cochlear implants who not only knows sign language, but also is able to hear sounds. In this shift, we learn a new way to listen to God, and we begin to listen when God is speaking instead of merely asking God to speak when we feel like listening. We learn to ask the questions that God is answering, rather than merely asking him to answer what we are already asking.

Before the shift, we ask, "What does God want me to do?" After the shift, we listen to what God wants us to become.

Before the shift, we ask, "God, give me a sign" because we long for God to decide for us. After, we notice how God strengthens our wisdom and discernment to decide for ourselves.

Before the shift, we want God to give us more options and open doors. After, we want him to limit options and close doors.

Before the shift, we ask that God would make our decisions successful. After the shift, we allow God to set us apart, so that we might be more like him in our decisions.

Finally, before the shift, we inform God of our plans and ask him to move through our efforts. After shifting from Ask to Listen, we look for what God is already up to in our world, and we listen for how we might engage ourselves where he is already moving.

Yes, God's agenda takes longer than ours. But by asking better questions, we will get more precise answers that will last longer than the quick and easy ones. Instead of praying, "Lord, what should we do?" we could ask, "Lord, what is important to you?" The answer to the first question may get us through the next few weeks. The answer to the second question will shape us for the rest of our lives, and we'll get the next few weeks thrown into the deal. Instead of asking, "Who should we marry?" we could request, "Lord, teach us to love," and the matter of who to marry will soon take care of itself. When we ask who to marry, we are asking from our agenda. When we ask God to teach us to love, we are asking from his agenda, and his is truly the better agenda. Until we know how to love, it probably doesn't matter who we marry. After we know how to love, we can choose to marry among many but with the right empowerment to make the marriage actually work. Instead of asking, "Lord, why are we in this mess?" we could ask, "Lord, how can we bring honor to your name in this situation?" Once again, the second question is larger than the first, yet it is not a completely different agenda. It encompasses the first, just as God's agenda encompasses our own.

So we have a choice to make. We can deal with God like a Magic 8-Ball, ready with a shake to tell us what to do. Or, we can have wisdom to listen to the Father's noiseless voice and learn to ask for whatever he is telling us.

We start out with our own agenda at our own time and expect him to speak in our language. But as we shift, we begin to let God speak in his own way, in his own time, and with his own agenda.

⤙

Right now, I (Dave) find myself typing these words at a perfect little writing retreat. It's a log cabin in the mountains, and my window looks out on the Blue Ridge Mountains. I can see all the way to West Virginia from here. Behind me, across the river valley, lies the beautiful Shenandoah National Park, where the Blue Ridge Parkway and the Appalachian Trail wind past a hundred stunning views. It's a beautiful thing to see.

But from where I sit, it's not a beautiful thing to hear. My three kids are one room over, and they're on vacation today, while I'm on writing leave. Just days from the end of school, they are bouncing off the walls, literally at times, as they launch off the couches. As any parent knows, no sound is quite so interrupting or irritating as children arguing, whining, or screaming at each other. Some common refrains are: "Stop touching me!" and "I had it first!" or even "He's trying to kill me." He's not, he claims. Her belly just happened to hit his fist, apparently. My wife's most hated whine is one that usually comes just minutes after finishing lunch: "I'm hungry; I want a snack."

However, I have a secret in the midst of this din. Right before this vacation, I purchased some noise-cancelling headphones. I've seen people use these on airplanes and looked at them before, and I thought they might be a gimmick. But they work! Usually, when listening to music on earphones, I can still hear the kids in the next room: "She won't stop taking my Legos!" This defeats the purpose of the earphones. But with these new, noise-cancelling headphones, I can flip a little switch and tell the difference immediately. Somehow, magically, they shut out all the noise, and I can only hear whatever I'm trying to listen to.

We need something similar when listening to God. We need some noise-cancelling times. Prayer is such a time. There is so much noise in our world today. The noise of entertainment is constant. Television, radio, and the Internet used to be something you deliberately used. But now, with portable devices, we have trouble shutting things out no matter where we go.

Like bloodthirsty wolves, our e-mails, texts, calls, and posts pursue us at every moment, never allowing us a moment's peace. Instead of paying attention to one another, couples text other people from bed right before going to sleep. I (Dave) once overheard a guy watching a YouTube video in the stall next to me in a public bathroom. Not long ago, at my favorite restaurant, I saw a girl whose parents had taken her out to eat to celebrate the end of her semester. All throughout the meal, her phone (which I suspect they were paying for) kept ringing. She answered every time, carrying on long conversations about the most vapid issues. I was there next to them the entire time, and they never really had a conversation with her.

This is how it is with God. There he sits with us, longing to communicate. He would celebrate us and inspire us if only we would disconnect with the other voices in our lives to hear his voice. Henri Nouwen writes: "True listening has become increasingly difficult in churches and institutions, where people remain on their guard, afraid to expose their weaker side, eager to be recognized as successful or bright. In our contemporary, competitive society, listening often is a way of 'checking the other person out.' It is a defensive stance in which we do not really allow anything new to happen to us. It is a suspicious way of receiving that makes us wonder what serves our purposes and what does not."[4]

The key is not to get God to speak up—it's to get the world to shut up. Do you have ways to do that? What serves as your noise-cancelling device in your routines of life? Do you have a special time and place when you get alone? If not, you should. Do you have methods that help you focus and hear from God? If not, you can. Do you know how to shut out the din and hear from him? If not, you will. That's what it means to move from Ask to Listen.

How do we discern God's voice? There are a few methods that have worked for us. First, when God speaks, it is always consistent with his Word and nature. He doesn't tell you to do things that are contrary to his Word. He'll never command you to be prideful. He never allows you to hold a grudge of unforgiveness. If a voice is telling you to break one of the Ten Commandments, you're not hearing his voice; you're just hearing voices. God has never said, "Go ye therefore and commit adultery and bear false witness while you're at it." This may seem obvious to you, but we have heard of many people who committed adultery on the premise that "this is the one God has for me; I married the wrong person." Many people have misled others because the person they were trying to hurt was a bad person. But God never speaks in these ways. They are a sure sign you're not hearing from God. God is unchanging in his holy perfection, and he never advises you to do something less than that.

Second, God's voice is also consistent with the way you and I tend to function. For instance, I (Steve) usually take a long time to make important decisions (spending a lot money, hiring new staff, and so forth), so when God speaks to me, I have noticed that he usually works far in advance. He gives me a sort of shot across the bow, a circumstance, offer, or chance conversation that requires no immediate decision but that sets me up for the decision that has to be made later. You might say that he aligns things into a constellation so that, looking back, I am able to know what he wants me to do.

Other people always make their decisions in the company of friends, and so God carefully surrounds them with wise people long before they have to decide anything. Some people have to feel it before they can make a decision, so God tends to develop their feelings, curiosity, or level of comfort long before they have to decide. Still others need to feel nothing. They are doers who trust their instincts or ability to analyze the data, so God tends to subtly remove from their menu of options any alternative that could ruin them. By the time they even see their options, they can only choose between good, better, and best. The choice between good and evil has been taken from the menu. God knows the way we start to change. He knows what will hook us—a new action, a new emotion, or a new thought—and he leverages this to shift us.

❧

Sometimes, God speaks to us through our circumstances. Earlier, we told you about Earl and his decision to move to Ohio. There's more to the story. Many years later, Earl's friend and partner wanted to start a different company, so Earl bought out and became full owner of the auto parts company. Things went very well for him as owner—so well, in fact, that he had a buyer interested in the company after just a few years. It was a competitor of his that was much larger but that couldn't seem to penetrate the region and was beginning to lose clients to Earl. In those situations, the competition usually continues for years. But, flush with new capital, the company came to Earl with an offer he couldn't believe.

In most years, he wouldn't have even flinched and would have rejected the offer. "The sky is the limit for this company," he thought. And even though he didn't start the company, after nearly twenty years there and eight years as owner, it had become his baby. He initially said no, but the competitor said, "The offer stands on the table. Let us know if you change your mind." Earl wouldn't budge. His friends and business associates agreed with this move when they heard about the offer. They thought it might not be enough money. Earl was thinking the same way.

Not long ago, Earl and his wife went on a mission trip to Pakistan with a group of people from their church. It was life transforming like he never thought it could be. Earl saw poverty and oppression he never knew existed. He met kids who had no shoes and saw schools where five kids shared one school book. He met a farmer whose family was starving and said he just needed one hundred dollars to get seed and hand tools in order to get back to even again. Earl couldn't believe how far his money could go over there. He talked about the experience to everyone he saw when he got back. He started to fund efforts in that country left and right and even sponsored five Pakistani schoolchildren.

He wanted to do so much more. Their church was going to help fund building a new church and school in one mountain village where some had converted to Christianity. But the fundraising had been difficult. He had already given some money to that, even sacrificially, but didn't have many more assets to tap.

That's when Earl and his wife started to think about the offer for the business differently. Talking about it seriously just a few months after being so sure they should not sell was a bit of a shock. But as they began to talk, they both felt almost immediately that the time was ripe. They knew that if they sold, they could contribute more than ever and still live comfortably, even if he had to find a middle-management job somewhere else. So they started to talk to others about this idea, and that's when they felt a strange vibe from everyone. Every single person they talked to thought it was crazy for them to sell the company.

However, their leading was very strong, and they sold the company outright. They were completely convinced that God was providing an opportunity for them, and in their prayers, they had an enormous peace, even though no one else supported the decision.

About six months after the deal closed, the economy in their region tanked. Looking in hindsight, there was no better time for them to sell. He heard that one of the vendors who had provided 25 percent of their orders went bankrupt and defaulted on nearly all outstanding payments. He realized that if they had held on to the company, they would have spent five or more years digging out of the hole to get profitable again, if ever.

Earl got out instead and got his money. But, it was his money for only a time. Most of it went to Pakistan. With the help of Earl's money, they built that school and church, and then went on to lead their church in building five more schools and a hospital in the next four years, along with countless new water wells.

People still ask Earl, "Boy, you got out at just the right moment—how did you know?" He always says, "I didn't know. God knew, I guess. He just happened to convince me to do something more important."

Finally, God sometimes speaks to us through our impulses—not always, but sometimes. Have you ever hopped up and down on one leg in the soda pop aisle because God told you to? We haven't. However, a friend of mine (Dave) heard of a woman giving a peculiar testimony.[5] She was driving one morning on the interstate. She sensed in a strange way that she should stop at the next gas station, and a wild idea came into her mind: she should go in to that place and hop on one leg in the soda pop aisle.

At first, she ignored the idea because she didn't want to be late, and because, well, it's somewhat insane. But as she passed the exit, she sensed very strongly that she had made the wrong choice: "Really, God, can you seriously want me to do something so crazy?"

She made a U-turn and drove up to the gas station. She walked inside, noticing a nineteen-year-old kid at the counter. No one else was there. She was glad, since this was going to look very weird. She stood there in the soda pop aisle, and she raised one leg and hopped on the other for about ten seconds. Nothing happened.

She just shrugged her shoulders at God and started to head back to the car, trusting the kid at the counter hadn't seen her. But then she caught him staring at her with a strange look as she passed. "Why in the world were you doing that?" he asked. Sighing to herself, she said, "Well, I don't know, to be honest. Maybe I'm just nuts. I felt like God was telling me to come in here and do that. Don't worry. I'm leaving now."

The kid smiled but in a painful sort of way. "Lady, you're not going to believe this, but my life is in shambles. To be honest, for the last week, I've been thinking about killing myself. It's that bad. And I've worked here all night long, and I've been planning to go home and end it all. I prayed about an hour ago, the first prayer I've prayed since I was little, and I said, 'God, if you're real, and if I shouldn't do this, then you've got to stop me. I won't kill myself if you send someone in here who stands in the soda pop aisle and hops up and down on one leg like a crazy person before my shift ends.'"

To follow our impulses can be a dangerous practice. After all, people have done some evil things on an impulse that God told them to do it. But we mustn't let a few sinister people keep us from listening to the quiet, subtle impulses that may come from God on any given day. Most of them are not radical or revolutionary moments. In fact, the more radical the impulse, the more we should cross-examine it with other things like God's Word and his people. But most of the time, it will not be the fear of doing something evil but rather the fear of looking crazy that will keep us from trusting our impulses. But if we can risk it, if we dare to look silly in the soda pop aisle every now and then, perhaps there are still more things that God wants to tell us through our impulses.

❧

God speaks to us in a variety of ways. No matter which way God chooses to speak to us, there's only one answer we should give: Yes!

When I (Dave) was a small child, I had an odd experience. I was so young that I don't remember this, but my parents told me about it later. They were up late watching television, and I walked into the living room in my pajamas with the feet in them.

My parents were amazed to see me walking so wide awake that late into the evening and wondered why I was up.

I said, "Mom and Dad, God is speaking to me."

And with no hesitation, my father replied, "Go, tell him 'Yes.'"

Once you hear from God, "Yes" is the only reply. We want to hear from him. That's for sure. But are we ready to say yes? Are we ready to listen and do whatever he asks?

Do you hear voices? The good kind, that is? The voice of God? You never know what he might want to tell you. It could change your life.

REFLECT AND WRITE

In what ways has God already made shifts in your soul from Ask to Listen? Write your story and testimony of what God has done in you.

How might God be calling you to shift from Ask to Listen in the coming year? Write what leadings God is giving you or impressions you received during this chapter.

ASK TO LISTEN QUESTIONS

SOULSHIFT QUESTIONS YOU ASK YOURSELF

What is the difference between asking someone something and really listening to them?

How might you learn to pay better attention to someone?

What patterns do you have in your life for God to find and speak to you?

SOULSHIFT QUESTIONS YOU WILL NEED TO BE ASKED

What obstacles make it hard for you to really listen to others?

How could you restructure your quiet time (such as, your devotions) for God to more clearly reveal himself to you?

Think about the last big decision you made. How did you make it and who helped you? What part did God have in helping you decide?

SOULSHIFT QUESTIONS YOU WOULD DISCUSS WITH OTHERS

What types of activities make it possible for people to really listen to one another?

What role does this group have in helping each of us know the will of God for our lives? What role could it have? What role must it never have?

How could we design our time together in this group to better hear and know the voice of God?

6

SHEEP TO SHEPHERD

a shift in influence from following the crowd to leading like Christ

A man can't just sit around!"

So said Larry Walters.

Everyone who heard this laughed. Everyone, that is, except the air-traffic controllers of the Los Angeles International Airport.

Sitting in his lawn chair one day, Larry decided it was time to fulfill his childhood dream. Armed with a CB radio, pellet gun, camera, and sandwiches, he tied forty-five helium-filled weather balloons to his lawn chair and started floating over his backyard. His intention, he said, was to hover at about thirty feet over his yard, take some pictures, and then to shoot the balloons—one at a time—until he dropped slowly to the ground. But when his friends cut the anchor, Larry took off. Higher and higher he went. Within minutes, he was soaring at fifteen thousand feet and drifting away from his neighborhood.

After sailing for forty-five minutes and wildly out of control, Larry finally had the courage to shoot his first balloon. Then he shot another, then another and, just as he expected, he slowly descended.

The LAX air-control tower received a report from an aircraft taking off. The pilot allegedly reported seeing a man in a lawn chair at fifteen thousand feet. The tower thought he was kidding until they saw Larry for themselves. Larry had drifted over the controlled airspace of the airport. Within minutes, he was tangled in power lines and, with some help, was able to climb to the ground. He was arrested immediately, and when the cops asked why he did it, Larry said, "A man can't just sit around."

Larry was later fined fifteen hundred dollars for his little escapade and was given a prize at the Bonehead Club of Dallas and an honorable mention in the 1982 Darwin Awards.

To be sure, his tactics were a little far out. (Do we need to emphasize you should not try this at home?) However, there's something to his statement. There comes a time when you can't sit around any longer. You have to do something. And that time comes for everyone. There is a moment—at least one—in people's lives where they are called to summon their courage, to find a way, to seize the moment, to do what is right, and to take as many with them as they can. But that moment is subtle, unpredictable, and unannounced, so it is quite often squandered because of fear. Even while we long to do something crazy, to make a mark on this world, we want even more to fit in.

One day, Moses was out watching his people work as slaves in Egyptian brickyards when he noticed an Egyptian beating a Hebrew. Since Moses was a Hebrew who had grown up inside the pharaoh's own palace, he knew firsthand how annoying some slaves could be. He owed his life to the powers of Egypt. He must have been glad, as all Egyptians were, for the work of Israelite slaves. As a boy in the palace, he had certainly enjoyed the benefits of their slavery. But here was something different. Here was a cruel injustice. Here was an Egyptian beating the life out of a Hebrew, and Moses, the man between two loyalties, was caught in the moment. He must have wanted to turn away. After all, it was not his battle; it was not his problem. If the Egyptian had killed the Hebrew, there surely would have been witnesses, and systems were in place to deal with the killer. Sure, let the system take over. Let the professionals handle it. It will all work out. It always does.

But Moses couldn't just sit around. There comes a time when you have to do something. You have to take charge of the moment. Most such moments will not be heroic. They may not even be noticed. But you have to do it because it is the right thing to do, because people need you, and because something bigger is at stake than your little fear. Some things are more important than fitting in. So, Moses slipped in behind the Egyptian, picked up a rock, struck him on the head, and killed him (Ex. 2:11–12).

It is important to note here that the Bible nowhere condones the action of Moses. Rather, the purpose of this story is to show how Moses' zeal against the oppression of his people got him into trouble. Douglas Stuart writes, "This was his first attempt at delivering his people—acting alone and in secret and relying on his own strength and wisdom—and though it failed miserably, it certainly shows the strength of Moses' sentiments on behalf of his people."[1] Moses' zeal here, while misguided and tragic, is the first sign that he is taking responsibility for the conditions of his people, which is why the story is reported at all. Alan Cole writes, "It was not Moses' impulse to save people that was wrong, but the action that he took."[2]

Some months later, another episode happened with an entirely different outcome. Seven women were out drawing water for their father's flock when a group of shepherds spotted them and drove them off. Once again, Moses got involved, running into the fracas and driving off the shepherds, this time probably using his status as Pharaoh's son to do it (2:15–17). And why? Was he attracted to the women? Was he stuck on himself? Or was it the same thing that drove him to kill the Egyptian months earlier? Was it patriotism? No, these women were not even Hebrews. If it was patriotism that drove him to kill the Egyptian, what drove him to do this? It turns out that Moses was a leader before he knew it. God had placed within him a capacity to look after the interests of others. Something inside him just couldn't sit around. Sometimes it is violent and sometimes very tender. But it has to do something. It has to take charge.

So when God heard the cries of the Israelite slaves and decided it was time for a change, he knew exactly who to use (2:23–25). A shepherd, named Moses, was on the far side of the desert, and he had already shown himself willing to take action. Now, when he needed a leader to take his people out of Egypt, God would summon from within Moses things that Moses did not know he had.

We often think of Moses as a fearless leader, but Moses did not think of himself as such. When God first called him to bring his people out of slavery, Moses balked. He went from "Here I am" to "Who am I?" to "Send someone else" (3:4, 11; 4:13). Many in leadership positions do not think that they have the gift of leadership.[3] But God is looking for unsuspecting people like Moses—maybe even the crazy ones like Larry Walters—the ones who don't just sit around like everyone else.

❧

Phil loved two things about his small group: (1) the pastor was the head of the group and he always led a great Bible study; and (2) a few of the ladies in the group baked some amazing pies each week. He often joked, calling it the "pie with the pastor" small group.

When the pastor went on vacation or to a conference, Phil led the group. When he led, it was always a real challenge—he had big shoes to fill. But he did it anyway, and the rest of the group insisted he did a great job. Phil always suspected they were somewhat relieved when the pastor came back from vacation.

But eventually, the situation changed. The pastor announced he was leaving Phil's church to be the pastor at another church in North Carolina. It was a surprise for the whole church, but for this small group, it was heart wrenching. They were such close friends with the pastor and his family. The pastor had even told the small group they were thinking about the change before he told the church board. They prayed for the pastor and his family—and they understood—but group nights were very hard. Everyone hated to see them go.

But for Phil, it was worse yet. The pastor took Phil out to lunch and told him that he thought Phil should take over leadership of the group in the pastor's last two months so he and his wife could just attend the group during the transition and so that the group would be prepared to go on without them. It was hard for Phil to imagine that kind of commitment. He was only in his late twenties, and he didn't have any theological or Bible training. But the pastor assured Phil that he'd give even more support to him in the last few months, and that he'd do a great job. With a little bit of training and the opportunity, the pastor said Phil could shepherd the group even better than he could. "You and I are both shepherds, Phil," the pastor told him. "I just have the whole church to think about, and you have this group."

⟵

You've been told that Christians are supposed to follow. You need to follow Christ. You need to follow the pastor. In fact, you are most likely quite good at following. You, like all of us, follow the herd. Follow the trend. Follow instructions. This is all well and good. Not harmful. Following is where it all begins.

We are familiar with computers, cars, e-mails, and cell phones. But most of the heroes of Scripture were more familiar with shearing wool, leading sheep to pasture and water, and defending these animals from predators. The people of biblical times knew sheep. Abraham, Isaac, and Jacob all tended them. Moses wasn't the only one who heard God's voice from a burning bush; his flock of sheep witnessed it as well. The sling that launched a stone to fell the giant Goliath was well practiced from years of fighting off the natural predators of David's beloved sheep. The prophet

Amos preached his sermons with a scroll of Scripture in one hand and a shepherd's crook in the other. God's people in ancient Palestine lived their lives, more often than not, with sheep.

Sheep are loved, and those who care for them are favored in Scripture. When God required the first acts of worship east of Eden, he asked for the sacrifice of a lamb, and when Jesus was born, the first and only people the angels announced it to were shepherds and their sleeping flocks of sheep on a hillside near Bethlehem.

With sheep as a normal part of daily life for the people of the Lord, it was a perfect way for God to express the relationship he would have with them.

We are his sheep.

- "We are your people. We are your very own sheep. We will praise you forever. For all time to come we will keep on praising you" (Ps. 79:13 NIrV).
- "Know that the LORD is God. It is he who made us, and we are his; we are his people, the sheep of his pasture" (100:3).
- "Oh yes, he's our God, and we're the people he pastures, the flock he feeds. Drop everything and listen, listen as he speaks" (95:7 MSG).

And God is our Shepherd.

- Jacob said, "Like a shepherd God has led me all my life" (Gen. 48:15 NCV).
- "Please listen, O Shepherd of Israel, you who lead Joseph's descendants like a flock" (Ps. 80:1 NLT).
- "He tends his flock like a shepherd: He gathers the lambs in his arms and carries them close to his heart; he gently leads those that have young" (Isa. 40:11).
- The psalmist felt the great care of God, providing for him and protecting him from danger, like a shepherd (Ps. 23).

Jesus even called himself the Good Shepherd (John 10:1–18). So following God like a sheep is a good thing. His people should be obedient and devoted and should allow him to lead them beside still waters and through the valley of the shadow of death.

However, at the same time, Scripture has a stream of instruction that calls us to become more than sheep. God calls us to be shepherds, to shepherd other sheep. Those in any leadership position must not lord it over those they lead (2 Cor. 1:24). Instead, the Bible teaches those in positions of authority to act like caring shepherds (2 Sam. 5:2), and he has no time for those who abuse that authority (Ezek. 34).

Jesus may be the Good Shepherd, but his disciples are called to be assistant shepherds, even while he is the head. In John 21:15–19, when Jesus and Peter had their first full conversation after the disciple's denial and the Savior's resurrection, Peter was eager to prove he was loyal again to his Christ. Jesus asked him if Peter loved him. At first, this must have been hard for Peter to hear: "Is the Savior questioning my commitment?" Jesus even asked him the question three times, echoing the three times Peter had denied him in the first place (John 18:15–18, 25–27). Peter was insistent: he loved the Lord, despite his prior denial.

When Jesus responded to this, he didn't say, "I know," or "Good, just checking," or even "I'm just messing with you, Pete." Instead, Jesus issued Peter a command: "Then feed my sheep" (NLT). Somehow, Peter could show his love by doing one thing and one thing only: feeding Christ's followers.

We can do the same. We can move beyond following the crowd as they try to follow the Savior. Jesus asks us to feed those he loves — to grow in our faith, beyond milk to meat, and then, when well-fed ourselves, to begin feeding others. This is the journey from Sheep to Shepherd each Christian is called to, no matter their station or position in life, no matter their gifts or graces. Everyone has someone to shepherd, even if you're a seventeen-year-old named Freddy.

❦

"You're the oldest, Freddy, so you have to be an example," his mom had always told him. He was seventeen years old, and his three younger sisters were fifteen, fourteen, and ten. Sam was the baby of the family at just four years old. Freddy had started to see how much his sisters looked up to him now that two of them were teenagers. They used to fight like cats and dogs when they were younger, and they still do in some ways.

One night, Freddy's mom and dad were out for a dinner function. The teens put Sam to bed, and then Freddy watched a movie with his sisters on cable. It wasn't the kind of movie they would have watched when their mom and dad were home. At first, Freddy felt a bit guilty, but it was a really good movie, and they were all getting into it. About forty-five minutes into the movie, it started to get violent. Freddy told Jennifer, the ten-year-old, that she had to leave. He figured that was something, at least.

But it was still awkward in the room as the scene started to get bloodier and bloodier. He started to wonder, "How much is in this movie? How far is this going to go?" So he got up and grabbed the remote, turning off the TV. He didn't have to say anything to his other sister who was there. She knew. So he sat down, and they just stared at the walls for a minute. That's when Bekka, who was fifteen, broke the silence by saying, "Freddy, why are we different than everyone else?" He was a bit irritated by the question. So he said, "Because we're Christians, silly."

She kept looking at the wall, thinking, and said, "Well, how do you know that?"

"Because we go to church and we're into Jesus and we read the Bible and all that stuff."

"I don't know, Freddy. I'm not sure I'm one."

He was blown away. What was Bekka saying? She did all the same stuff he did. Freddy said, "Do you mean you're doubting or something?"

"How do you know where you're at for sure? How can I know that I'm OK with God? I'm worried that I'm not."

"Oh, I see what you're saying. Well, I know that I prayed to receive Christ at that youth rally three years ago on Christmas break, so ever since then, when I wonder about that, I just remember that day. I wrote the date in the front of my Bible."

Bekka looked down, "That's what I mean, Freddy. I don't have a date like that."

This was definitely the strangest conversation Freddy had ever had with his sister. He couldn't believe she was talking this way with him.

"I wonder," Bekka continued, "maybe I should do something and have a date that could help me doubt things less. Maybe that would help me like it helps you."

"Sure," Freddy said. "That sounds like a good idea."

"So, what did you do, you know, to make it happen at that rally a few years ago?"

"Well, I just prayed the prayer the guy told us to pray and made a commitment."

"What did you say?"

So that's when he told her what he had prayed, and Freddy led Bekka to Christ that night. That's when Freddy started to realize that he needed to be a shepherd to his own sister. A whole new world opened up for Freddy, and the next world opened up for Bekka.

✦

A shift happens when you follow Jesus long enough that you begin to hear him say, "Go into the world. Heal the sick. Preach the gospel. Take up your cross." Before long, the call to follow Christ becomes a call to enlist in his service — to not only follow, but also to lead. It is a call to move from Sheep to Shepherd. Within your limitations and within your circles of influence (allowing only God to determine those), you assume responsibilities and take positions. You lead family, friends, even groups of people who are outside your comfort zone. God is calling you to step up into conversations and situations where you will be used—where you will be a shepherd to others. He might be calling you to start reading the Bible with your family, to volunteer for the first time in your church, to wonder about the spiritual climate in your office, or to start thinking about the spiritual life of your friends. He is calling you to lead while you follow. It might start with shepherding a child, even your own child. It might go so far as being a shepherd to a crowd.

It is much easier not to take on these responsibilities. But people experiencing this shift in their lives have often discovered that they are already responsible for those around them—the responsibility is not voluntary, it's a given. Those who live in this SoulShift have simply begun to take that responsibility seriously.

*

Once upon a time, two American hikers in Scotland came upon a hole in the forest. The hole was deep and dark. Looking over the edge, they had no idea how deep it was. One of them tossed in a small stick. They heard nothing. The other one grabbed a rock the size of a baseball. Tilting their ear to the hole they waited for a thud or a splash to signal how deep the hole was. No sound ever emerged.

Intrigued, the hikers shed their packs and started throwing larger items down the hole, hoping to hear a sound. They found a large stone and heaved it in together. No sound. They found an old iron sink from a junk heap nearby and threw this in. Again, nothing. Everything they threw in was swallowed and never seen or heard from again. The pit seemed bottomless.

Then they found a long, abandoned railroad tie nearby and, carrying the heavy object over to the hole, threw it down. They waited for some noise, but again, nothing. Suddenly, they were startled by a noise behind them. Turning around, they saw a wild-eyed sheep running right at them from a dense patch of trees. They both dodged away, and then were astonished to see the sheep run right at the hole and jump in. They couldn't believe it. They sat there stunned.

A few moments later a Scottish shepherd walked out of the forest up to the hikers. "Hey, have you boys seen a sheep of mine? He was around here, but I can't find him. He was my daughter's pet."

The hikers regretfully informed him that they had just seen a wild-eyed sheep run from the forest and into this bottomless pit, apparently committing suicide.

"Well, that couldn't be the one," the shepherd replied. "Our pet sheep was tied to a railroad tie."

Shepherding is risky business. There are all kinds of threats to the sheep we take into our care. Hopefully, no one will throw them down a bottomless pit, but there are dangers to be sure.

Our culture is a constant opponent in our journey to become more like Christ. The sheep in your family, neighborhood, workplace, or church are in need of all the things spiritual sheep require and that spiritual shepherds throughout the centuries have provided.

What should we do for the sheep under our care?

First, identify your sheep. You won't be able to care for a flock if you don't know who makes up your flock. If you have children, it's obvious that they are under your care. Where do you volunteer? Those you serve are the sheep in your care. What is your profession? Whatever it might be, those you rub shoulders with are those you influence. Do you lead anything? If you have a position of influence, no matter how inconsequential you might think it is, then you have a flock under your care. Who are your sheep? Think of those who informally come to you for guidance or advice. How might you shepherd them?

Next, be sure your sheep are fed. Ask questions about their spiritual diet. Learn what they are reading. Find out what questions they have about Scripture, and then search for answers together. Use your influence in their lives to ensure they are growing in God.

Sheep also need water. For spiritual sheep, this points to the need for community and relationships. Rare water holes and streams in Palestine had to be sought out. Shepherds had to lead their sheep to water to ensure they didn't dehydrate. Our sheep will dehydrate relationally if they don't connect with others. Spiritual sheep were not meant to live alone any more than real sheep were meant to go without water.

Protection is another need sheep have. The training David received as a shepherd prepared him for being a king. As a shepherd, he was not only concerned with providing; he was also concerned with protecting. He had already killed a lion and a bear to protect his flock. You try taking on a hungry bear with your bare hands! David was certainly able to kill Goliath with a rock. Our sheep need protection too. They need to be told where the predators are waiting. They need to know what kinds of entertainment might rob their identity. They need to know what temptations are around the corner and how God has provided an escape for them. Our sheep need to know someone will stick up for them in the real world and will pray for them before a real God.

⋘

In considering how to move from Sheep to Shepherd, perhaps the best thing is to imitate the example God gives us. In Ezekiel 34:11–16, God explains how he will care for his people — as a shepherd. At every turn, we can learn to shepherd others as he does.

Instead of hoping others will care for people, we should do it ourselves, for even God, "the Sovereign LORD says: I myself will search for my sheep and look after them. As a shepherd looks after his scattered flock when he is with them, so will I look after my sheep" (34:11–12).

Instead of letting obstacles or distance get in our way of shepherding, we can follow his example to rescue them from wherever they may be scattered. "I will rescue them from all the places where they were scattered on a day of clouds and darkness. I will bring them out from the nations and gather them from the countries, and I will bring them into their own land" (34:12–13).

We can find good places for them to feed on the Word of God, places for them to connect with us and other sheep. "Good pasture, and the mountain heights" provide what can only be described as "rich" (34:14).

When we haven't heard from people in some time or when they turn from God, we won't forget them. Like God, we "will search for the lost and bring back the strays" (34:16). We can, like God, ensure our sheep are getting the rest they require. "They will lie down in good grazing land. . . . [We] will tend [our] sheep and have them lie down" (34:14–15).

When our sheep have deep wounds in their psyche or when crisis has weakened their faith, like the Good Shepherd, we can "bind up the injured and strengthen the weak" (34:16). And we can speak the truth with love when our sheep stray from truth and succumb to sin. Like God, we can "shepherd the flock with justice" (34:16).

If you want to know how God wants you to shepherd his sheep, look to how God shepherds, and you'll have the perfect example. Do what he would do.

Alice couldn't believe she was nominated in the first place. She felt more than over the hill; she felt like she'd been over twenty hills, and she was so ready to retire. It seemed to her that the leadership of her church should be made up of younger people or at least people younger than her. But she wasn't just nominated; Alice was elected to the elder board of the church. On the first ballot, she was in, and she was surprised.

Alice was overwhelmed with this idea. She had never been in this kind of leadership capacity in the church. At their first elder meeting, she learned that she'd need to pray with people at the altar now, and even to anoint them with oil. "How strange," she said to herself. "I'm an insurance agent, for goodness sake, not a counselor or a priest." The other elders disagreed. They said that it was time for her to step up and be a spiritual leader in the church. They said she was respected and ready.

Alice realized they might face some really big decisions. "What if the pastor leaves, and I have to help find a new one? What about the financial crisis? What we do will affect all those employed by the church and the ministries for hundreds of people." She knew it was a lot of responsibility.

But it was time, past time in fact, for her to shepherd some other sheep in the church.

※

The idea of being a shepherd is a bit foreign in our culture today. The Western mind is more acclimated to the Wild West hero than the supposedly meek and mild shepherd. The Bible talks about the Good Shepherd. But we're thinking John Wayne and Clint Eastwood.

There's something about the American psyche that idealizes the cowboy image—the distant loner with a past. His confidence and intensity is at the same time intimidating and alluring. Women might roll their eyes about his macho act when he's not around, but when he's there in the flesh, they find themselves lost in his eyes. But you can't get too close. You know he'll be taking out the bad guy in a gunfight at high noon, and then riding off into the sunset at the end of the day . . . alone.

This Lone-Ranger-minus-Tonto image is one we're much more familiar with than that of a shepherd. The cowboy mentality is revered in other genres. What was the Han Solo of Star Wars but a cowboy who flew a spaceship instead of riding a horse? We even elected a cowboy movie actor as president of the United States. We like cowboys.

And shepherds have some things in common with cowboys. They spend their days leading animals through the wilderness, and they spend their nights under the stars. They both know how to deal with danger. And they're more at home in a canyon than a city.

But that's where the similarity ends. Max Lucado noticed this and described how different a cowboy and a shepherd are in his book *A Gentle Thunder*: "The shepherd loves his sheep. It's not that the cowboy doesn't appreciate the cow; it's just that he doesn't know the animal. He doesn't even want to. . . . Why the difference? Simple. The cowboy leads the cow to slaughter. The shepherd leads the sheep to be shorn. The cowboy wants the meat. . . . The shepherd wants the wool."[4]

The goal is different for a cowboy and a shepherd, so they each treat their animals differently. The cowboy's journey ends with the death of the animal. The shepherd's journey never quite ends—they live life with the sheep. The cowboy wrestles, brands, herds, and ropes the cattle. Cattle need to be driven to the destination. The shepherd leads, guides, feeds, and anoints. They lead the sheep to safety, not slaughter.

This is why, Lucado says, we can be glad that Jesus didn't call himself the "Good Cowboy."[5]

We must resist the temptation to remain sheep, but we must also beware of becoming cowboys. Our culture teaches us some bad habits in leading others. Instead, remember that the Good Shepherd's example is the one we are to imitate. God doesn't want us riding off into the sunset alone. He wants us to feed his sheep as if they were his because they are, after all, borrowed sheep. It's his flock we tend.

REFLECT AND WRITE

In what ways has God already made shifts in your soul from Sheep to Shepherd? Write your story and testimony of what God has done in you.

How might God be calling you to shift from Sheep to Shepherd in the coming year? Write what leadings God is giving you or impressions you received during this chapter.

SHEEP TO SHEPHERD QUESTIONS

SOULSHIFT QUESTIONS YOU ASK YOURSELF

Who is spiritually investing in you right now? What are they doing that is so valuable to you?

Who are you spiritually investing in right now? What else could you do that might be valuable to them?

What God-given skills and gifts do you have that could be shared with others and your church?

SOULSHIFT QUESTIONS YOU WILL NEED TO BE ASKED

What leadership opportunities has God opened for you in the past few months? How did you respond?

What are things in your personality that make it difficult for you to move from Sheep to Shepherd?

What relationships or friendships do you already have that you could perhaps shepherd more intentionally? What specifically could you do to step it up in that relationship?

SOUL**SHIFT** QUESTIONS YOU WOULD DISCUSS WITH OTHERS

How does our group make room for people to grow and develop their God-given gifts?

What could we do to restructure so that the weight of shepherding would be carried by more people?

Do we have people in our church who are not being shepherded closely enough? What role could our group have in helping them?

ME TO WE

**a shift in priority from
individualism to community**

ere's a trivia question for music lovers: What song has been so well-known for so long that both Elvis Presley and LeAnne Rimes covered it? Which song is so gritty that Johnny Cash and Willie Nelson growled through it on their records? It was timeless enough for Judy Collins and Joan Baez. It was spiritual enough for Chris Tomlin and Jars of Clay. It had enough folk appeal for an indie artist like Ani DiFranco, and enough slap-you-in-the-face honesty for the hardcore punk band Dropkick Murphys. But the song was sweet enough for viral sensation Susan Boyle to bellow it out. This song has enough soul for the Neville Brothers and enough majesty for the Mormon Tabernacle Choir. What song was recorded by all the above?

Answer: "Amazing Grace."

It was written in 1748 by John Newton at the moment he was gripped by God's love en route to Liverpool. His eyes were opened; he turned from his sin; and he wrote this famous and popular song.

And everyone lived happily ever after, right?

No. At least the slaves in the bottom of the ship at the time didn't. Newton was a slave trader, you see. He penned this beautiful poem of grace in the comfort of his cabin, while many Africans sat huddled—cargo in the bottom of the rocking boat. God's grace was amazing enough for Newton, but it didn't cause him to release the slaves. In fact, after the song was written, he boarded another ship and traveled from village to village, buying human beings. He then sailed across the Atlantic, studying the Bible in his quarters, while two hundred slaves were in the hull, shackled two by two, squeezed into shelves like second-hand books. Almost a third of them died during the long, torturous voyage. When they arrived in South Carolina, Newton delivered them to their new owners, knowing full well that they would finish their lives in hard toil and oppressive labor while he sat in church services and strolled through peaceful fields in the woods outside Charleston.

There are cultural sins that people in every country and era are blind to. Newton might have experienced the grace of God personally, but he was still blind to the sinful ways he engaged in. He bought into the assumptions of his day; he was so surrounded by and immersed in his culture that asking him to define slavery as sin would have been like asking a fish to define water. It didn't make it right. It was still sin. It was a cultural sin—one that millions committed at the same time.

Newton lived long enough to realize this as the abolition movement gathered steam and many leaders in the culture began to challenge the assumptions. Later in life, God's amazing grace redeemed Newton's view of slavery. Newton even later published a work called "Thoughts Upon the African Slave Trade" to support the abolitionist movement, where he, as a former insider in the human trade, described the actual conditions on slave trader ships like the very one aboard which he penned "Amazing Grace."

But first, he had to confess his sin—the sin of the culture, but one for which he too was culpable. He said it was "a confession, which . . . comes too late. . . . It will always be a subject of humiliating reflection to me, that I was once an active instrument in a business at which my heart now shudders."[1]

What might be the cultural blindness of our day? What stowaway sins ride in the belly of our vessel? In our day, we experience a grace one could only call amazing. But what cultural sins will surprise us in our old age? About what will we say, "I never knew"?

Our cultural sins may be many. Nearly two million in the world today are poor. A billion are hungry. Our slide into moral relativity has been quite imperceptible but significant. Our sex-crazed culture has produced a mind-boggling amount of pornography. It might not be a coincidence that the elderly among us have many concerns about the culture that they were a party to but now see with better perspective. And lest we forget, slavery is still with us. According to estimates, twenty-seven million people are trapped in the sex-trafficking slave trade to this day.[2]

However, that terrible list might not be the unknown cultural sin we're talking about. While these problems are horrific, we know about them. You might not have known the statistics, but you knew each sin as it was listed.

Let's talk about just one sin you might not see coming. This is a cultural sin that could be at the root of all the above problems, while many do not even consider it a vice. In fact, it is mostly viewed as a virtue.

The cultural sin most ignored today? Individualism.

If you're an American, this view of life is most entrenched. You grew up in a country that fought an honored war of independence, and you've learned to think just the way your culture has taught you. Here is how the doctrine of individualism works.

I am a loner, even if I like to be with people. Better to be a lone ranger than a long-time member. I am an army of one. I order my hamburger "my way." I have a very specific kind of cappuccino that suits me. I get off my iPhone and onto my personal computer where I log onto my blog or Facebook page which has a picture of me as its logo. At a writers' conference, Leonard Sweet referenced the Nintendo motion sensor video game, pointing out that we are so individualistic that we now use two *I's* to spell *we* (as in "Wii").[3]

In my religion, I am a denomination of one because I have personal beliefs that I've made up my mind about. I have a personal relationship with Jesus Christ; I read my Bible alone; and I have my own version of truth. When I leave church this Sunday, before I wonder whether the service was good for everyone else, I will tell you whether or not I liked it, just as I do when I leave a movie theater. I give it my personalized thumbs up or down.

I have individual rights. I am sovereign over my own choice and my own body. My rights extend even to the death of another I may carry in my womb.

Have you noticed how I've used the word *I* around fifty times already in the above description? We are overly self-conscious, perhaps even self-ish and self-obsessed. The Internet has changed from a place where we find information to an arena for talking about ourselves. We have obscure Facebook groups for people who confess they "use the word *like* too much." But so far there are no groups who confess they "use the word *I* too much." We compulsively update our status or tweet our thoughts, the subject of which is usually the same: me. Yet, so far, there is no Facebook group called "I talk about myself too much." There is a group, however, called "I secretly want to punch slow-walking people in the back of the head." It has more than 10,000 members![4]

In his book *Making Room for Life*, Randy Frazee talks about the way our neighborhoods have changed with this culture. Years ago, houses were built right next to each other, with big front porches, short driveways, and side-walks that stretched from house to house. Neighbors sat on their porches more than in their homes and carried on spontaneous conversations with those who walked by. But today, they build decks on the back of their homes with remote door openers for garages that are connected to the house. Back yards have privacy fences. Dogs are used to discourage a friendly knock on the door as much as to deter thieves.

It is no accident, says architect Philip Langdon, that "the very moment when the U.S. became a predominantly suburban nation, the country has suffered a bitter harvest of individualized trauma, family distress and civic decay."[5] In 1974, nearly one-fourth of Americans visited with their neighbor several times a week. By 1994, that figure had dropped to 16 percent, and there was a shocking increase in the number of people who had "never spent an evening with their neighbor"—from one in five to nearly one in three, a 41 percent increase.[6]

Adele Gaboury's neighbors knew who she was, and you might say they took good care of her. When her lawn grew hip-high, they paid a local boy to mow it down. When her pipes froze and broke, they called to have the water turned off. When the mail spilled out the door, they called the police to clean it up. Her car, full of trash, was towed at one point as a fire hazard. The only thing they didn't do was to check on her; they never knocked on her door to see how she was doing with all this going on. They reported later that, technically, they hadn't seen her in quite a while, so they didn't even know if she was alive.

Well, she wasn't.

Police discovered this when they climbed the crumbled stoop to her little blue house and forced their way in. There were the seventy-three-year old skeletal remains in a five-foot-high pile of trash, where they had apparently been for almost four years.

How could this happen? Neighbor Eileen Dugan put it well: "It's not really a very friendly neighborhood" she said.[7] Yeah, we might have guessed.

Eileen, who at one time was close to the deceased Adele, went on to confess, "I'm as much to blame as anyone. She was alone and needed someone to talk to, but I was working two jobs and I was sick of her coming over at all hours. Eventually I stopped answering the door."[8]

Who answers the door when you knock? And for whom do you answer the door when they knock? Who is your community?

You need a place to go when you've hit the wall, and people with whom you can celebrate accomplishments. You need people who are there for you when you need help, prayer, or advice. There needs to be a group of people in your life who don't pressure you to pretend to be something you're not. And when you're moody or erratic—they know you're just in a phase; they don't give up because of one time when you blow it.

It goes both ways. You must love these people so much that when something happens to them, you have to be there or you lie awake all night. You want to witness their shining moment or shoulder their heavy load. There are people whose disease you would gladly take from them if only they could live longer. Who are those people for you? Do they exist? Whom could they be?

✍

Gina moved to the Northwest U.S. in order to go to college this past year. Much of college life was new for her, but most of those things she could see coming. What took her most by surprise was looking for a church. She liked her home church, but she took so many things about it for granted. All first semester she visited church after church, eventually going to ten different ones. The churches in her new area were nothing like her church at home. She didn't know what it was about things in the Northwest, but the churches all seemed so lifeless to her. Since none of the girls in her dorm went to church, it was tempting to just bail on the idea and go to the Wednesday night campus ministry she had heard about and call that her church.

While Gina was home for Christmas break, she read about the church in 1 Corinthians and had an epiphany about what community is. She realized she needed to commit to one of those churches she had already visited, warts and all.

She decided to go to the church that was closest to her dorm. It might not have been the worst in the bunch, but it wasn't the best either. The music was quite rusty, the preaching left her a bit confused, and she wasn't sure if the people were as friendly as they should have been. She won-

dered if it might have been because of her appearance: She had a nose-ring
a   n   d
jet-black dyed hair.

But that first week, she was determined to be committed no matter what.
They had a sign-up sheet in the lobby for the ushers, who were recruiting
new members for the team. She showed up to their orientation meeting that
Wednesday night. It was pretty hilarious. She was sure they had no idea
whose name was on the list, and when she appeared, they thought she was
lost and needed directions somewhere else. It was all middle-aged, white
men and then little Gina. There was only one woman other than Gina there.

But a cool thing happened. They appreciated her spunk and took her
under their wings. One of their wives asked her to come over for Sunday
lunch nearly every week. One week they had an usher team lunch at her
school's cafeteria, spouses included.

That's when some of Gina's friends came up to her and asked who all
those suit- and dress-wearing people were. She told them the story, and
they looked at her funny. "Are you serious, Gina? You're an usher at that
old church?"

They all laughed about it then, but several of Gina's girlfriends are now
going to that church. Their favorite thing is to find the door she's posted at
and, when she hands them a bulletin and greets them, they think it's so
ironic and funny. They were all there when she stood up with several other
families and became a member of the church in April.

⋘

The apostle Paul would have believed firmly in Gina's decision to join
her church. He once told a parable to make the same point. "In one body
we have many parts," he said, "so we who are many form one body in
Christ" (see Rom. 12:4; 1 Cor. 12:12). Paul was speaking to the Corinthian
church he knew so well. The members of the church were living mostly
independent lives. They quarreled, competed, and complained. They min-

imized each other's views and experiences—or ignored them altogether.

When it came to spiritual gifts, it was most problematic. The most respected ones in Paul's little church were those who could lead up front and not just the preachers. There were some who could speak in tongues and others who could interpret them. There was a middle-aged couple who could heal; a few of the board members believed they could perform miracles. Everyone knew who they were. "I don't feel like I'm included in this church," some would think, "because I can't do what they can do." A few of the elders even agreed and supported this separation between the "elite" Christians and the ordinary ones who, they figured, were needed only for their money. The ordinary folk were content to visit the church they attended and stay on the margins. They put their names on the newsletter list and maybe brought a dish to the potluck every now and then, but they mostly stayed to themselves. Yes, Paul's little church was a church of individual Christians who gathered on Christian soil.

So, Paul sat down and fired off this parable: In my body, there are hundreds of parts. Somewhere outside of those parts, and yet inside of them, is a mystical force that unites them so they are all a part of Christ. They all act like him. They all defend him. They all serve him. If one of those parts, say a foot, were to go rogue and complain, "Because I am not a hand, I do not belong to the body" (1 Cor. 12:15), it wouldn't stop being a part of the body. It would simply be an inactive part of the body (12:16). If the whole body were just one hand, or a bunch of eyes or ears, it could not function. Before a part of my body can serve the whole body, it must defer preferences, agenda, and glory—its entire identity—to the rest of the body. That goes for the more popular parts, too. It turns out that those parts of the body that seem weaker are actually indispensable (12:22–23).

Now ask yourself, "If my hand belonged to my body the way that I belong to my church, what use would it be to me? If my eye communicated with the rest of my body the way that I communicate with the rest of my church, would I see anything?"

A noted physician once took Paul's parable a step further: "The analogy conveys a more precise meaning to me, because though a hand or foot or ear cannot have a life separate from the body, a cell *does* have that potential. It can be part of the body as loyalist, or it can cling to its own life. In fact, some cells do choose to live inside the body, sharing its benefits while maintaining complete independence." This physician then pointed out the two medical names these separate cells are given: either parasites or cancer.[9] Nearly everyone everywhere believes the church is not what it should be today. Perhaps the number one reason is the parasitic and even cancerous effect that so many of us who have not moved from Me to We are having on the body.

The ongoing trouble in Paul's little church was that its members saw themselves as individuals dissimilar to the whole. They felt peculiar. Different. When that happened, they began to see their gifts and resources as distinctive, something that separated them from the herd. Instead of wondering how their particular gifts contributed to the whole, they emphasized how their particular gifts were different from the whole, or better than the whole. But to be a member of the body, said Paul, is to be someone "who is willing to be accountable for and committed to the well-being of the whole."[10] The opposite of this was to be a user or a client who uses the whole for one's self.

The shift from Me to We involves using our gifts for the sake of the common good. Mature Christians are always asking themselves, "What is in my hand that might be useful to the common good of the body where I belong?" They share their power and glory. There is a certain humility about them. They don't worry about how they stack up against other members. They aren't too conscious of their positions because they have accepted the arrangements God has made for them in the body.[11] What some consider politics, these people consider providence. They accept the structure and convictions of those around and over them. They defer to the body the right to shape their convictions and determine each member's role in serving it.

How many people do you know who truly belong to anything like Paul did at this little church? Most "members" today are not really members at all. They are in the database, and they sit in a pew once in a while, but they are not members of the body like Paul described. Or they do things up front for themselves—hogging glory instead of distributing it, being seen but not truly belonging. These independent ones do not belong to their churches the way they expect their eyes to belong to their bodies. On the day they discover this and seek to truly belong to their church, a momentous and seismic shift has occurred in their souls.

❧

Desmond Tutu, the influential African archbishop, wrote a book called *God Has a Dream*, in which he talked about the idea of *ubuntu*. The concept is prevalent in many African cultures and flows from the Bantu family of languages. Tutu tried to nail down what this concept means in the book by saying, "You know when ubuntu is there, and it is obvious when it is absent. It has to do with what it means to be truly human, to know that you are bound up with others in the bundle of life."[12] The Me to We shift is about being present in the only place where ubuntu can become more than just a nice philosophy: the church. Christian community is the best hope for a world where ubuntu shows up and stays, whether you're in Africa or Alaska. From Austria to Australia, the church is the best shot we have. Whether you live in Albania or Argentina, it does not matter. The church is where it's at, or where it is most likely to be found in reality. The church is the right soil for the ubuntu seed.

When you seek the advice of others; when you allow them to help you interpret the meaning of God's Word for your life; when you allow them to set the moral standards that you and your community practice; when you develop your spiritual gifts in order to serve the greater body; when you accept the correction of others—when these things happen, you are bound up in the bundle of life. You are shifting from Me to We and are being transformed. This is one of the reasons membership matters for you in a local church. Becoming a member is not a way for you to be in the club. It's not a way to gain certain benefits or for you to get certain positions or a discount in the rental fee for your daughter's wedding. It's a formal process of moving from Me to We.

Tutu later clarified his thoughts on the Me to We meaning of ubuntu by saying, "My existence is caught up and inextricably bound up with yours . . . A solitary human being is a contradiction in terms" and "You can't be human all by yourself."[13] In the shift from Me to We, you do not abandon your identity; you actually discover your true identity for the first time in the body of Christ.

The Bible paints God's picture of how he wants these relationships to function in your life. When you move from Me to We, many things happen.

You accept the other person without passing judgment on them (Rom. 14:13). You use your gifts and talents to care for another person's needs, not just for selfish gain or self-expression (1 Cor. 12:24–25). You carry other people's burdens (Gal. 6:2).

Your celebration and mourning is not just for your own wins and losses. Beyond those, you also rejoice with those who rejoice and weep with those who weep (Rom. 12:15). You pray for those who are suffering and sing songs of praise with those who are cheerful. You might even go so far as to anoint the sick with oil and pray for them (James 5:13–15).

These relationships aren't of shallow tolerance. They are the place you can speak the truth in love (Eph. 4:15); and then confess your own sin in return (James 5:16); and, when someone else confesses, you meekly restore them to God's dream for their lives (Gal. 6:1).

Rather than competing for power and position, and instead of just doing what you want or holding to your own personal convictions, you actually defer your rights to the weakest members of the body (Rom. 14:1). Their convictions become yours somehow. And more than merely doing all these things yourself, you're compelled to encourage others to do good works as well (Heb. 10:24).

⤜

The carry-in meal, the pitch-in, the after-church potluck—whatever you call it, this phenomenon is perhaps one of the greatest inventions of humanity. Everyone comes together bringing their favorite dish and you get to sample everything you love and avoid what you don't.

One time, I (Dave) remembered at the last minute that I was invited to a potluck. I panicked. What would I do? Usually my wife plans a wonderful dish to represent our family, but this time I was going alone, and I hadn't prepared anything. I rushed out to the corner market and searched like a stray dog in an alley for something to grab. I quickly snatched two packages of cookies off the shelf. "Everyone likes cookies," I thought.

When I arrived, I was overwhelmed with the wonderful smells of home-cooked food. Some families had cooked things in Crock-Pots for a whole day. A few old ladies had made their legendary pies. One guy brought a giant cooler full of his special sweet tea, which I would be able to sip on all afternoon.

There I was in the doorway—tie askew, dress shirt untucked, late, and my contribution to this festival of food was two packages of store-bought cookies. I should have been thrown out.

Instead, I was greeted warmly. With apologies, I shrugged, showing all I had to offer, confessing that I had forgotten. I cracked a few jokes about how my wife was usually in town and helped me look like less of a schmuck. But I was accepted anyway.

I went over to the dessert table where all sorts of sweet and gooey madness was displayed by a dozen loving hands that were trained by their great-grandmothers how to roll it out, how to put it in jars for winter, and how to use the perfect amount of sugar, flour, and time. In between the cakes, pies, and creative works of art, I nestled in a package of oatmeal raisin and sugar cookies that I could tell were rock hard. I don't even like oatmeal raisin cookies. The meal went on as normal, and no one noticed who had brought what. I might have brought the finest thing on the table for all anyone knew.

At the end, as everyone was retrieving empty dishes and leftovers to take home, I assumed my lousy store-bought cookies would be unopened. I was surprised to see someone had pity on them and me, opening the packages and taking some from each.

Even the paltry items I brought were taken. Even I had contributed. The sweet-tea guy passed by as I gathered up the remains and said, "Hey, those ones weren't bad. I love oatmeal raisin cookies!"

This is how community works. This is how fellowship happens. Yes, the food part is important to fellowship. But authentic life together is like this even without the potluck. We all feel that what we have to contribute is not enough and will not be valued. But we are accepted anyway.

In a perfect world, we are loved for who we are when we come, and then encouraged to grow along the way. Even if all the gifts you bring to the table are stale or store bought or used up. Even leftover people are loved. And what's more, you get to partake in a feast unparalleled. I say this is a "perfect world," but it happens in a variety of ways all the time: You walk into a church with next to nothing but are ministered to and perhaps even given to before you give anything. You walk in on the verge of a marriage breakdown with no advice to give anyone other than, "Don't get married till you're ready because I wasn't." And then the group gathers around you and lets you feast on their marriage wisdom, saving your marriage in the process. You join a class on Psalms at church, knowing nothing about the subject, and walk out with a bunch of learning on loan, and a new love for the poetic prayers of Scripture.

The head of the body, Jesus Christ, animates all believers as a community. "Just as our bodies have many parts and each part has a special function, so it is with Christ's body. . . . We are many parts of one body, and we all belong to each other (Rom. 12:4–5 NLT). The parts of the body "should have equal concern for each other. If one part suffers, every part suffers with it; if one part is honored, every part rejoices with it" (1 Cor. 12:25–26).

If Christ is in us and we are in him, the community we become functions like one great big welcoming potluck, where whatever you bring to the table is received and whatever is already on the table is yours for the taking. We "clothe [ourselves] with compassion, kindness, humility, gentleness, and patience. Bear with each other, and forgive . . ." (Col. 3:12–13). This sounds like a party in a perfect world, but it is one that is possible, that has already happened in every age since Christ left us behind as his body, and it is still happening today. This is the joy of moving from Me to We.

Anne Lamott tells the story of a little girl who got lost one day. She ran up and down the streets of her city, terrified, looking for landmarks she would recognize. There were none. Eventually, a police officer found her and offered to drive her around until she recognized a neighborhood or a street. As they drove around, they came upon the little girl's church, and she said, "You could let me out now. This is my church, and I can always find my way home from there."

Lamott adds, "And that is why I have stayed so close to mine—because no matter how bad I am feeling, how lost or lonely or frightened, when I see the faces of the people at my church, and hear their tawny voices, I can always find my way home."[14]

So can you.

REFLECT AND WRITE

In what ways has God already made shifts in your soul from Me to We? Write your story and testimony of what God has done in you.

How might God be calling you to shift from Me to We in the coming year? Write what leadings God is giving you or impressions you received during this chapter.

ME TO WE QUESTIONS

SOULSHIFT QUESTIONS YOU ASK YOURSELF

How connected do you feel to your church? Is this more or less than at other times in your life? Why?

How has the body of Christ around you influenced you over the past few years? How have you grown or changed because of your association with them?

What next step would make your commitment to your church more meaningful?

SOULSHIFT QUESTIONS YOU WILL NEED TO BE ASKED

Who are the people who have helped you the most in your spiritual life? What rights or what power have you given them?

If you were to have a SoulShift coach, what would you like or need him or her to do? Specifically, how should he or she coach you?

What is your greatest fear in making a more tangible or meaningful commitment to the church?

SOULSHIFT QUESTIONS YOU WOULD DISCUSS WITH OTHERS

Does our group or ministry encourage or discourage people from belonging to the church? What should be the relationship between our group and the rest of the church?

How does our ministry or group support and work with the good that already exists in other areas of the church?

What could our group do to inspire more people into a greater ownership of the church? What other rituals or functions (besides membership) might help them to gain a better appreciation for the body of Christ?

8

NOW WHAT?

Have you ever noticed those maps they have in the mall? You know the ones: kiosks with a big, multicolored map with each store labeled on it. One time, a teenager stood at that mall map, staring intently at the little red dot, the one that says, "You are here." Seeing the designation, she said, "Wow . . . that's amazing. How do they know exactly where we are?"

If you have ever been lost, having someone tell you where you are is the key. A handy map of where you want to go is helpful too. Good directions are a bonus. However, it all starts with that "you are here" moment.

You've got problems, just like everyone else—stuff you try to solve. But at your core, you have one spiritual problem that is more important than all others. Your number one spiritual problem could be stated this way: Where am I right now, and how do I get where I want to be? If you know the answers to those two questions—present location and next steps—things will start to change, and you'll begin to grow as God wants you to.

The previous sections were intended to give you a clearer sense of the first question. As you consider each SoulShift, you can more accurately push a pin into the map and say, "I am here." You can say, for example, "I have a long way to go on Me to We, but this has been a year of immense growth for me in Consumer to Steward."

There was once a businessman driving around in the hills of West Virginia, utterly lost. He stopped at a corner gas station where the old attendant sat in the sun, half asleep in a lawn chair. The businessman leaned out the window and said, "Excuse me sir, but I'm going to Harristown, and I seem to be lost. How would you get there from here?"

The old man got a strange look on his face. His eyebrows met and he became thoughtful. His eventual reply wasn't helpful, "Buddy, you sure are lost bad. If I was going to Harristown, I certainly wouldn't start from here!"

Well, guess what—you have to start from here. You have no choice. You can't start five years ago—before something in your life happened. You can't start five years from now—after whatever is coming up soon. Your soul has to start in this place and this time.

Here. Now. Shift.

STUFF HAPPENS

For more than a year, I (Dave) played cards at a local bar and grill one night a week. The people who hang out there on Tuesdays are a bit different than the people pastors typically have as friends. Perhaps you connect with unchurched people at your place of work.

Life is complicated. It's messy. The lives of my Tuesday night friends aren't necessarily pretty. Let me tell you about one of my best friends there. I'll call him Ben. He works long shifts at a loading dock in town. He called me one night to say he might not be able to come over to my house for a

Friday night get-together because his wife had left him and the kids, and he wasn't sure he had a babysitter. I was freaking out; I didn't see this coming at all. Things seemed fine with them last I checked. But it was complicated. She had cheated before, and he suspected that was the case again.

I saw him the next Tuesday night, and I asked for more details. What was going on? His first reply was just the introduction to a long story, but it pretty much summed up everything.

"Dave, stuff happens."

Well, he knows I'm the kind of Christian who doesn't drink and smoke and cuss like a sailor. Ben was editing his language for me a bit. You've seen the bumper sticker and know the real word. "Stuff happens" was a good edit for me.

Stuff does happen, doesn't it? Stuff has happened to you. Bad stuff, no doubt. And stuff will happen again. You don't know when. It might be five years or five weeks away, but stuff happens all the time. It's hard to be ready for it.

Part of the SoulShift process is planning ahead. It's about looking forward to the coming year and considering what you might do to grow in Consumer to Steward, for instance. Or you might say, "I want to make a more intentional shift in Me to We, and because of that, I'm going to join a small group Bible study, even though I've always given excuses for not doing that."

That first part is huge. Being intentional (what you see coming) is a big part of what you can do to make the shift. But along the way, stuff happens. For instance:

- Your mother might need to move into a nursing home.
- Your boyfriend might break up with you.
- You might get laid off.

All kinds of bad stuff might happen. You won't see it coming until it happens. And good stuff might happen that you don't see coming too:

- Your oldest child and your grandkids might move back to town.
- You might get a promotion and bonus at work.
- You might get engaged to your sweetheart.

The unexpected good and bad stuff happens. Your plan to grow and shift in certain ways might go to the sidelines in these seasons. This is not a bad thing. God is still in control because when big stuff happens, God still wants you to grow.

In fact, those are perhaps the most important times of spiritual growth in your life. The bigger the stuff, the bigger the shift that needs to happen. Each of the above examples is not just stuff happening—each is an opportunity to shift your soul.

❧

Our staff at College Church was talking about the idea of SoulShift, considering how we might communicate this life-changing spiritual development idea to the church. It was a very serious meeting. It was the perfect moment for one of the chuckleheads on our staff to crack a joke, as this person is prone to do.

The staff member said, "I need you to know that I shouldn't be the one to make a public announcement about SoulShift. I just know that I would jumble up those words and make a mistake, and then a video of me saying a cuss word is going to be all over the Internet the next day, and I'll regret it the rest of my life."

The meeting exploded into laughter at this point, as everyone started to think of the mistakes we could accidentally make. Then another staff member (also a chucklehead) blurted out, "Shift happens."

I (Dave) was unable to get control of the meeting after that. In fact, yet another chucklehead staff member (yes, we have several, me included) went home and used iron-on letters to make a T-shirt that he wore into the office the next morning. On the front it said, "Shifts Happen." I'm working hard to restore order and make the appropriate SoulShift to regain decorum in our team. But, enough about us. Let's talk about you.

Stuff happens in your life: there's a death in the family, you are diagnosed with cancer, or your parents get divorced. When these life-changing bad things or even significant good things happen, something else can happen that's even better. In fact, the best time to shift is during the worst and best stuff of life. Think about the last season when you really made key decisions and changes in life; it was likely during a key time of stress or crisis. God uses these seasons. Shifts happen when stuff happens.

It is hard to fully shift from Me to We until you've felt utterly alone. When you've hit the rock bottom of loneliness, you truly start to need others and become willing to enter into true community. You learn to submit to others, to the sometimes-feels-crushing love of parents or spouse or congregation.

Nothing quite makes you shift from the Seen to Unseen until someone you love dies. The other world becomes so much more real once someone you know leaves here and takes up residence there.

Many people shift from Me to You when they have a child. At some point, you have to become selfless to survive parenthood. Crying babies in the middle of the night don't give much back (except cute pictures once in a while).

You can go right down the list of stuff that might happen and find the kind of soul-shaping change that could happen afterward. You cannot usually plan for these kinds of shifts. They don't always come at the time you'd like to make them. However, in God's providence, he gives you the hand you're dealt, and it's your turn to shift. If you use the shifts as a paradigm to think of how you can grow, then whenever stuff happens, you will be ready to turn that stuff into the kind of shift that restores your soul.

PACKING FOR THE ROAD

Nobody does road trips quite like my cousin Scott. He puts me to shame. When I (Dave) go on a road trip, it just means some suitcases are tossed into the hatch of the minivan, a coffee mug goes into the cup holders, kids go into the car seats, and we're off. We'll be gone maybe five days. But when Scott takes the family on a trip, it's like a Pentagon-planned mobilization. Instead of just leaving for a week, they may go for six weeks at a time. Scott does much of his work for World Hope International on the road, so he'll just take the family with him for months at a time, crisscrossing the states much like Forrest Gump's random run.

Scott's wife, Elizabeth, homeschools their four boys, so they all go along. They prepare well for their time on the road. They load up into a mobile home and strap on all kinds of bikes and gear on the back. They have all their school supplies along and every toy, tool, book, or utensil they will need for the days on the road away from home. At first, I thought maybe Scott was forcing his family into this harebrained scheme—but no, the rest of the family set me straight when I questioned it. They once spent the better part of a year on the road, and all six of them said it was one of the best years of their lives.

It amazes me to see this family live life on the road. Their home goes with them everywhere they go. Can you imagine living like that?

In a way, you already do. You're on a spiritual transformation journey, and it's a long trip. You can't go back to the beginning to pick up what you forgot. You're on a road trip with many shifts and bends in the road, so it pays to be ready for whatever comes up next.

Now we need to talk about what you'll need to take along on the trip. You've read about each of the seven shifts. The shifts might be most accurately called the destinations of your journey. The first word in each shift is a hint at where you've been and where you are. The final word in each shift is a hint at where you're going and how you need to get there. You've been a Sheep before; now, you're becoming a Shepherd. The Seen was all you saw until you caught a glimpse of the Unseen realities. You've Consumed and now begin to Steward. These are the spiritual outcomes that define transformation.

However, you'll need some inputs in your spiritual formation to ensure you get to your destination. The *SoulShift* philosophical approach to transformation emphasizes the outcomes of spirituality; they begin with the end in mind. However, we don't want to minimize the importance of righteous input in your spiritual walk. When you do your devotions or say your prayers, when you go to church or go on a mission trip, when you confess your sins or take Communion, when you do any number of spiritual disciplines or activities—these are inputs of great value. They are what you take along and use on the road trip of spiritual transformation. We want to help you plan for the trip, making sense of what to take and how to get where you need to be going.

GETTING STARTED

Now that you've worked through this book, you have a better sense of where you are in your spiritual life. If someone you trust asked you, "How is it with your soul?" you might be able to give an answer.

However, your map doesn't just include a starting point; it includes a destination. You're going somewhere from here. Where is that? What is your plan?

You can certainly do a lot of different things now. You could try to tackle all of this, and perhaps you have the energy and time to give specific, intentional attention to all the shifts all the time. Or not.

Perhaps like most of us, you need some priorities, some starting points. When you consider where you're at in the SoulShift (how you've assessed yourself), in what intentional ways would you like to grow most in the coming year? By next year at this time, where do you hope to be?

These are not really goals as much as areas to invest your time. It's choosing which categories to keep in front of your mind. If you do this, a few things will happen.

GOD MAY INSPIRE YOUR CHOICE

You could end up picking a shift or two in which you didn't even know how much you would need to grow. God knows what's coming, but you don't. So he may inspire your choice in ways you will only spot later. Sounds like something God would do, doesn't it?

GOD WILL ORDER EVENTS

He will give you opportunities to grow in that area. These things might have happened anyway, but you'll at least have a new perspective on how to grow with them in your life. It is possible, however, that God will respond to your choice by giving you more opportunities and tools and resources to use in that area. Vickie, one of our church's worship leaders, calls these "God Echoes." These are the times when God's activity echoes throughout your life in multiple moments. Listen for them. His voice certainly does have a loud and long echo.

GOD WILL CONVICT YOU

You may forget your choice of a SoulShift. You will likely put this book on the shelf with others you read once upon a time. You will get caught up in other things. But while reading Scripture, in reading the paper, during times of prayer, while driving your car, at a worship service, at work or even on vacation, when everyday life continues in these ways, the Holy Spirit will bring it back up to you. If you commit now to shift more fully in these ways this year, then he is not going to let you off the hook so easily. Count on it.

So, now it's time to choose—time to fall off the log one way or another. What SoulShifts will you make a priority in the coming year? Write them here.

A SPIRITUAL ROADMAP

OK, that wasn't so hard, was it? Now, *SoulShift* is all about the outcomes you want in your life. As we said before, it's beginning with the end in mind. This is good. This is the point. However, many inputs into your life can help or harm you in your shifting journey. What you put into your soul affects your soul. You need an intentional plan moving forward. This roadmap is written by you for you. What do you think you should do to shift in those ways? Do you need somewhere to start? Use the following chart as a guide to write your map of the road ahead.

SoulShift	Keep Doing	Stop Doing	Start Doing
Write below two SoulShifts you're targeting in the coming year and why you feel you should grow in these ways.	What are you already doing well in these SoulShifts that you should keep doing or do more often?	What are things you are doing that prevents you from growing in these SoulShifts and that you will stop doing? When you will stop?	What will help you grow in these SoulShifts that you will start doing this week? Write how often you will do it.

You have to fuel your life in order to take this journey. You'll run out of gas along the way if you don't make spiritual pit stops. The spiritual disciplines are inputs, and *SoulShift* is about outputs. This is a good thing because, in the end, you want to be focused on Listening and the Unseen. The We and the You become more important than the Me. You should become a Child and a Steward and a Shepherd. But you can't just magically make these shifts without the right inputs. There are practices, experiences, and disciplines that God has commanded you to do and that Christians throughout history have modeled for you.

KEY PRACTICES

Many key practices are obvious to you, because we talk much about the spiritual disciplines in the church. But just doing spiritual disciplines doesn't necessarily shift a soul. God must guide the shift in your heart. And you must also aim the spiritual discipline inputs toward the SoulShift goals God wants to make in you. Don't just check them off your mental list on a daily, weekly, or annual basis. Instead, as you engage in each spiritual discipline you've done for years—or perhaps start engaging in new ones to broaden your spiritual experience—be sure to have in mind the shifts God is causing in you or calling out of you. Then you'll be pouring this vital spiritual fuel into your tank, rather than spilling it randomly all over the place without purpose.

In looking over the following list of spiritual discipline inputs, make notes as to how you might adjust your current practices in these disciplines or how you might start new ones to foster the shifts of the soul you are targeting this year. Feel free to leave some of these blank because you do not need to engage in every one of the disciplines at high intensity every year. (But don't consider the ones you don't like to be optional. You may need to stretch this year by choosing one that's new to you.)

Disciplines of Abstinence[1]	Your Use of This Fuel
Fasting—giving up meals to pray	
Silence—listening to God but not speaking	
Solitude—getting alone to hear God	
Simplicity—purchasing only the necessary or living sacrificially	
Rest—giving a break to your body and soul and devoting that time to restoration	
Secrecy—not taking credit for giving, serving without reward	

Disciplines of Action[2]	Your Use of This Fuel
Journaling—writing down what you are thinking, hearing, and learning	
Hospitality—hosting others to make them feel better connected and honored	
Confession—speaking your sins to others and asking for forgiveness	
Scripture—reading the Word of God, hearing God's voice, and applying it	
Charity—developing a heart of giving through tithes and offerings and to those in need	
Prayer—bringing your private praise and petition to God	
Penance—doing restitution for wrongs by making them right	
Disciplines of Association[3]	Your Use of This Fuel
Community—connecting with others in a smaller group of sharing, caring, and learning	
Prayer—hearing and participating in the public prayers of the corporate church	
Scripture—hearing the Word of God read among his people in worship	
Presence—anticipating and experiencing God's movement among people	
Testimony—hearing or giving a testimony of God's work in the soul of an individual	

Disciplines of Association	Your Use of This Fuel
Conversion—publicly turning from sin and committing one's life to Christ for salvation	
Baptism—publicly confirming one's commitment to Christ and becoming a new creature in him	
Eucharist—participating in the Lord's Supper as a means of grace	

FOUR KEY HOURS OF THE WEEK

Other people have more money than you. They have more experience, more connections. They have more books or more smarts or more degrees. Others may have more friends or more support. But there's one thing you have the same amount of as everyone else: time. Everyone has the same twenty-four hours a day to work with. Yes—we all have different demands in life, but the sun rises and sets for you at the same times as everyone else in your town.

You may have heard it said that there are two ways to know what's important to someone: look how they use their wallet and their calendar. The wallet part is another subject (you can talk to God about that when you focus on the move from Consumer to Steward). But here we want to talk about your calendar and how you use your time.

Now that you have a roadmap for your spiritual shift this year, how are you going to structure your time? Maybe you have a computerized or handheld device calendar you love. Just type in the important things from your spiritual calendar. Or perhaps you carry a calendar in your purse or have one hanging on your wall. If so, mark matters of the spirit on it in a different color ink, so that it becomes a plan for the road ahead.

Bottom line: Use your time and enter the spiritual priorities of the coming year first. Your New Year's resolutions—the biggest priorities really—

should be more than just your waistline. (However, now that I think of it, that may be a part of Consumer to Steward as well.) You could start with two key steps.

If you don't know where to start in structuring your whole year, then start with a typical week. Like many other congregations, College Church is simplifying things by asking our people to give God four hours a week. The following are four simple words to help people order their week around the key priorities of life for a Christ-follower:

- Worship. The first hour means participating in a worship gathering with the congregation.
- Connect. The second hour means joining a smaller gathering of Christians in a class, group, or study where you can connect more deeply.
- Serve. The third hour means using your gifts and abilities by serving in the church and community.
- Reach. The fourth hour means investing intentionally in those who are farther from God and helping them make their next step.

We are sure you'll agree that all four hours of this list should be on your calendar. Are you the kind of person who goes to church and Sunday school and you attend very well, but you're not serving or reaching? Put those on the calendar too. Perhaps you reach out all the time and serve at the local community center, but you don't have a church home you're invested in and you don't have Christians you're living life with. If so, put that on the calendar this year.

Make sure each of the four hours is a part of your life on a regular basis and don't get out of balance. For example, someone who goes to seven Bible studies a week and two Sunday school classes but refuses to volunteer in the nursery or at the rescue mission is out of balance. You might call that spiritual gluttony.

The other key thing to do in structuring your year is to use special events or seasons to boost your spiritual energy. When you take a spiritual retreat or a vacation day to be with God; when you go to an inspiring concert or spend a week at a Christian camp; when you really engage in Lent or go on a mission trip—when you do these kinds of things, they can give you a spiritual boost. When you start to wind down spiritually throughout the year, be sure to schedule some key moments of soul reenergizing.

OK, now you've loaded up your spiritual mobile home with some good stuff for the road ahead. You can review your list to ensure you haven't missed something crucial. (By the way, a Bible is quite important to take along. If there are no Bible-reading pit stops in your plan, then you are going to break down pretty soon.) However, at some point, you're going to need to get in the vehicle, start your spiritual engine, and back out of the driveway. It's time to get shifting up the transformation road.

KEY CONVOS

Conversations are where shifts are sealed. A sermon might be good, a portion of a book might help your soul, but a conversation seems to seal the deal so often. You need to hear someone else and be heard by someone else—someone who can really know what you mean, someone to whom you can relate, someone who can even call you out from time to time, some-one who might be able to tell when you're exaggerating or leaving key parts out of the story, someone who has been tempted in the ways you've been tempted. These are relationships by which to shift.

We call the spiritual growth conversations you have with a SoulShift coach, an accountability partner, or a spouse "key convos." Every once in a while you need a key convo in order to shift yourself forward spiritually. If you're not sure how to start a key convo or how to respond in one, you might get a picture in your mind of two guys talking in their garage on a Saturday afternoon. Their names are Eric and Don.

"Hey Don, how's it going?"

Several lawnmowers are running in the background, and Don is running a piece of sweet-smelling cedar through his table saw, not hearing Eric shout out. Eric has to poke his head in the garage, knocking on the wall a bit to get his attention.

"Don, what's up bud?"

"Oh, hey Eric. Sorry, man, I didn't even see you there." He sets down his saw and takes off his safety glasses, "What's going on?"

Eric comes half-way into the garage, looking around at the walls of tools. "Hate to interrupt you, Don, but could I borrow your post-hole digger? The wife wants me to put in this huge bird-feeder she bought on eBay, and I think I'll have to put the monster in concrete."

"For sure," Don pulls it off the wall. "I haven't used this one in a few years."

"Thanks. So, what are you building today?"

Laughing, he says, "Oh, it's going to be a monstrous bird-feeder for my wife, of course!"

"Nice one. Seriously, what kind of Norm Abram–style marvel of wood-working are you producing this weekend?"

"Yeah, right, Eric. It's just a new mailbox. I'm sick of that rusting metal one."

"Yep, I've got the same one, but I think I'll keep it another decade until I buy a plastic one!"

Don laughs, and then asks, "So, where were you on Sunday, man? Did you get tickets to the game or something?"

"No, but that was an awesome game, wasn't it? I saw it on Phil's new sixty-inch LED. Wow, I could see the sweat on the linebackers' noses. You watch it? What an ending."

"Yep, it was great. Um, Eric . . . I think you know why I was asking. Remember, you had asked me to check in with you about Sundays and all."

Eric smiles, "Yeah, sorry — you caught me changing the subject again."

"Hey man, I wouldn't bother you about it if you didn't ask me to. You need to be on me about my stuff too."

"Totally . . . I haven't asked you some of those questions you wrote up in a month or so. Maybe we should go to coffee or something this week."

"That would be great." Don starts to get out some sandpaper and work the edges of the piece he just cut. "Now that I think about it, I wouldn't want you to ask those Me to You questions right about now! But I've made some great progress on the Steward one."

"Of course, 40 percent of your income is still going into tools, I see. When did you get that new drill press? Holy smokes, that thing is beautiful!"

"Uh, well, I told the missus that it would pay for itself in four years. We kind of made an exception."

"Yeah, Don, well, it's no skin off my back—the more extra tools you get, the more I get to borrow." Eric makes a big pointing motion at the wonderful post-hole digger he's holding in the other hand. "I only wonder about it because you told me about the money problems."

Don puts his safety glasses back on. "Yeah, yeah, I know, but I'll throw some numbers at you. It's been a good turn-around season for us, for real."

"Well good. I'm glad. About those Sundays you asked about . . ."

"There's been more than one?"

"Yeah, I know I need to be committed to it and all, but I've just been so busy. I know you're right, and I need to readjust my priorities. I'll explain more at breakfast."

"Monday work?" Don pulls a carpenter's pencil out of his overalls to write the day and time on a two-by-four scrap he pulls out of the sawdust.

"For sure, 6:30 at the pancake house as usual?"

Don finishes writing, and then says, "Yep, I'm there. And this time I'll remember to bring the questions you gave me. I'm asking all of them this time!"

"OK, thanks again for the post-hole digger."

Don just waves that it's nothing and is already powering up the table saw for another cut.

Eric and Don's conversation is an example of a peer conversation about SoulShift. These guys get together every once in a while to check on each other and have a key convo about the shifts they each want to make that year. But it's not the only kind of conversation that builds a relationship by which to shift. Eric and Don's conversation feels like an accountability-style convo. But oftentimes it's hard to keep those conversations going. It may be that you should start with someone you can go to who is mostly asking you questions. This is often someone older than you, but it should at least be someone you respect and seek out for wisdom. An accountability partner might be enough for you. Or you might want a SoulShift coach. Let's talk about what that might look like.

SOUL COACHING

Don't you hate it when your car breaks down far from home? I (Dave) drove two different cars cross country and both times they broke down. The first time, I was a nineteen-year-old college student, and my buddy and I decided to drive to California in order to go surfing. As pale freshman Midwesterners, we were convinced we would be naturals once we got some surfboards. The only problem was my buddy didn't have a car, and all I had was a Suzuki Samurai. If you've never seen one of these cars, it's basically a small imposter of an off-road vehicle. I had given it the name PseudoJeep. If you never owned a car in your youth that was bad enough to give a mocking name, you missed out.

So, my buddy and I drove across the country: plains, Rockies, desert, and Sierras. And we made it to the ocean. By then, my buddy missed his girlfriend so much that we turned the PseudoJeep east and started for home, never having surfed at all. But my PseudoJeep was more of a drive-around-town kind of car, so it started to break down in multiple ways. Most notably the engine began to scream at us. And when I say scream, I do mean scream. It sounded like a cat had become trapped in the gears. Every hour we drove, the screaming got worse and worse. We were toast.

In the dry highlands of California near the border of Nevada on the way back, we pulled into the only car place in the whole county: a Ford dealership.

It was Friday at 4:45 p.m. With Memorial Day coming on Monday, the mechanic was no doubt looking forward to a long weekend starting in fifteen minutes. Instead, he saw two stranded, clueless, college kids pulling up in a Japanese-made car with a screaming lawnmower engine. On top of it all, he noticed the license plates.

Him: "Did you guys drive this thing all the way from Indiana?"

Us: "We wanted to go surfing."

Him: "This thing isn't designed for that kind of trip."

(Engine continues torturous treatment of imaginary cat.)

Us: (Staring blankly . . .)

Him: "Of course it was going to break down."

Us: (Shrugging shoulders . . .)

Him: (Rolling eyes . . .)

It wasn't pretty or cheap. But eventually, after I emptied my bank account, we got the PseudoJeep home. I'm still not fully sure what was wrong with it. I only know it cost me five days stranded and thousands of dollars. I don't know what he did to the engine that week, only that he could have pretty much charged me anything, and I would have paid it. I didn't have anyone to give me a second opinion or any other way home.

The next time I broke down on a cross-country trip, it went much better. The reason: my father-in-law. This time my wife and I were on a honeymoon tour of the entire western United States. The only problem was the car. Near Spokane, Washington, the car started to sputter and putter and quit every time we pushed the gas pedal. It was odd. It wouldn't shift into gear properly, so it would skip and jump and so on and so forth. However, my wife's father is the quintessential car guy. And I don't just mean he changes his own oil. This guy sold cars for years and is a drag racer. He owns five or six racecars and even has people to drive the cars he built but doesn't have the time to race. So, when we started having engine trouble, we called him from a pay phone.

After I described the situation, he asked if the car was running. It was, right next to the gas station pay phone. He then said, "OK, hold the phone up toward the engine and step on the gas." Again, I just shrugged my shoulders and did so. The engine roared to life and then the puttering and sputtering happened. I got back on the phone, and though I don't remember the details he said something like, "OK . . . here's what you might have going on there. Take it into this and that kind of shop and ask them to check this and this and maybe even this. It shouldn't cost you more than about this much."

Wow. This experience was much better than the one I had in the Pseudo-Jeep. We had it repaired in no time with minimal cost because of his car-problem coaching. What was the difference? First, he knew what to listen for—even over a pay phone. And second, he knew what to tell us to do—in just one short conversation.

Someone should know your soul like my father-in-law knows my car.

That someone should know what to listen for, even on the phone. You need someone who knows what to tell you to do next. This person can be hard to find, but it starts with a few key steps from you.

HONESTY. Start by being honest that you don't know everything. At times, we are all clueless spiritually, just like I (Dave) was clueless about the car trouble.

OPINIONS. Convince yourself that you need a second opinion. You can't diagnose all your spiritual needs by yourself. Some people can just listen to your spiritual engine over the phone and figure things out quicker than you can. Call this person your SoulShift coach.

NAMES. Think of some names. Who are some people you already know who are good listeners and could be possibilities for a coach?

PERMISSION. Give someone permission. You'd be surprised at the good advice even some of those in your life right now would give if you just told them it was alright to do so (and no, we're not saying you have to go to your in-laws for this spiritual advice).

ADVICE. Follow that person's advice. You don't have to become a robot, think for yourself. But there's no need getting the second opinion spiritually if you're not going to take it seriously. Use the expertise and wisdom your coach gives to your advantage.

CONVOS. Build a routine conversation into your life with your SoulShift coach. Don't just say, "Well, I'll go to my coach when I need to." Unfortunately, when you need advice the most, you might avoid scheduling a time. Routine spiritual maintenance questions will expose problems before there are breakdowns.

QUESTIONS. Equip your coach with questions to ask you. In a spiritual conversation with the SoulShift coach you select, give him or her a list of questions to ask you. You can start with the questions in the chapters on each shift in this book. However, you can come up with more questions as unique as you are. This part helps grant your coach permission, but also equips him or her to ask questions you know you need someone to ask you. This will make the conversations get to the point more quickly and then be more effective.

We began this chapter by having to ask where you are now and how to get where you want to be. You do have to start where you are, but in this chapter, we've discussed all that is at your disposal in such a road trip. You can shift ahead in life when stuff happens. You can prepare yourself by engaging in key practices and by having key convos. The four key hours in the week provide the launching pad for such experiences, and a SoulShift coach can be a wise advisor in the process.

So, what should you do now regarding a SoulShift? You should start shifting. Each of the above practical steps could be your first step toward a significant shift of the soul in the coming year.

LEARNING TO FLY

Welcome to Duckville!" As you crest the hill, your tour guide waves a wing expansively to the quaint village of Duckville, USA, that five hundred domesticated ducks call home. Your feathered friend waddles awkwardly down Main Street, laboring to keep up with your stride. He points out each key historic and miniature building on the route.

You see Donna Duck's Impeccable Hairdressing Shop, "where a roost of female ducks is already having their plumage pampered on this lazy Sunday morning." Next you see Daniel Duck's Mallard Molting House, "out of season at the moment." You see Dewey Duck's Tapestry Shoppe, Dorothy Duck's Teahouse, and for a long while, you munch on fudge when you stop in at Dana Duck's Undeniably Delectable Desserts.

Then your wonderful tour guide explains that, to the right, you are seeing the jewel of Main Street and the oldest building in Duckville: the historic

Pigeon Post, where any duck can send a message around the world to long-lost friends and family by carrier pigeon.

This is when you stop your new friend among the talking fowls of Duckville. "But wait, good sir, why would you ducks need to keep pigeons who fly? Why don't you fly to these places yourselves to bring messages?"

The duck waddles over and looks at you with a smirk, "Well, of course there are a few who enjoy the old legends of ducks that could fly." Your tour guide explains the background. "Our ancient lore in Duckville includes many references to the Migration Myths of old, where ducks would take flight. However, we all know that ducks cannot fly. There are some who are inspired by these grand stories of ducks who were so free to do amazing things. But even they know they are just stories. The Myths of Migration are retold each Sunday at the Disciples of the Duck Deity Church over there." Your tour guide motions to a beautiful New England–style, white church with a pointy steeple on the hill at the end of Main Street. "If you are inspired by such myths, then we should visit the service that has just begun."

As the service reaches its climax, the duck disciples waddle around in their pews, quacking their hearts out to the duck Deity on the chorus of "On Eagle's Wings." Then David, a duck deacon, steps to the podium to give the sermon. There, he waddles back and forth on the platform, quacking out a rousing and fiery retelling of the duck Doctrine of Transformation about a duck just like them who jumped off a cliff, spread his wings, and flew into the clouds. The male ducks of the congregation puff out their chests in pride and the female ducks all have a tear in their eyes. As is the tradition, David the deacon duck repeats their creed: "We can be different; we don't have to waddle anymore; God has given us wings to fly. So fly, little ducks, fly!" And all of the ducks say, "Amen." Another deacon duck by the name of Dale waddles forward and leads them in an inspiring version of "I'll Fly Away."

Then, just when you think the ducks will retake their Deity-given flight, the service ends, and all the ducks waddle out the door, shaking each deacon duck's wing on the way out. Then, each duck waddles back home for Sunday dinner; even the deacon ducks don't fly away.

Your tour guide explains, "You see, these are wonderful stories. We value our traditions but we don't really believe ducks could ever fly. I mean, why did God give us these wonderfully webbed feet, which are designed for the water. The duck Deity doesn't expect us to fly!"

The flightless residents of Duckville are a lot like us. This Sunday, most of the one hundred twenty million Americans attending church will waddle home after hearing a sermon about flying. They will hear grand doctrine about the good life, about loving others, and about getting over their sins. They will say, "Amen," and then leave pretty much the same. They'll recite creeds and nod at sermons and even quack along on a few inspiring songs. But they don't really believe God expects them to fly.

Those in our pulpits are like the old preacher who once scolded his bedraggled flock saying "Look! This is my third straight sermon on being transformed. Why do you look like the same old bunch?" Those in the pew are wondering the same thing. Why indeed? Why do most of them not have the name of a single person in mind whom they are praying for and would love to see come to Christ (Me to You)?[1] Why do fewer than one out of six have a relationship with another believer through which spiritual accountability is provided (Me to We)?[2] Why do eight in ten say that they do not regularly feel as though they have entered into the presence of God while they worship (Ask to Listen)?[3] Why do fewer than one out of ten tithe (Consumer to Steward),[4] and only one out of four allocate any time during the week for serving other people (Sheep to Shepherd)?[5] Why do we want to be different but don't want to change?

It is not because we aren't serious about our faith. It is because we have not been taught how to fly. The deacon ducks keep telling us every week, but they cannot articulate what it means to actually fly, and they have not taught us how to do it. Therefore, we do not even believe it is possible.

One of the most powerful motivations for change is the sudden discovery that maybe we can. Change is possible. This is not the same as believing we have to or that other people want us to. It is way more powerful than the shallow belief that we should. To believe that we can begins as a whisper—a deep, quiet, subtle, and preposterous idea. It's an idea planted by God that causes turbulence at first, and soon rises as a tidal wave of desire, capable of altering everything on the landscape of our lives. Indeed, this whisper, this turbulence in the soul, will not quit until we have truly changed. SoulShift is not a change we have to convince you to make. The Holy Spirit has already convinced you or is still working on your heart. All we have done in this book is to give labels to his inklings. We didn't invent this. God did.

We've met our fair share of people who wanted to be different. For more than thirty years, in small and large churches, in my office and hallways, I (Steve) have counseled, led, and preached to Christians who wanted to be different. For more than fifteen years, in church plants and large churches, in dorms and with other pastors, I (Dave) have done the same. Most of those we've met with have promised to make radical adjustments in their lives. Some said that they were going to start a new discipline or break an old habit or join a small group. They had visions of being more content, more devoted, more balanced, more outgoing. They really wanted to be different. Some of them really did become different. Some of them changed.

Most of them did not. More often than not, they were no different than before. It wasn't because they didn't mean business or honestly desire to be different. It was because it's too hard to change or they didn't know how. They tried for a while and when their new enthusiasm hit the wall, they settled down into a pattern or a place and more or less accepted it as the new normal. They wanted to be different, but they didn't want to change. Perhaps more accurately, they didn't believe they could change. They came to believe it wasn't possible.

❦

But it is possible to change. God has a dream in mind for you, and all throughout Scripture, he paints a picture of what he wants you to become.

The future you is what this book has been about. We've written to people who want to be different but find it hard to change. As we have seen, most of us who say we want to become better Christians cannot define what it means, and so we don't know how to do it. That's where a SoulShift can help.

In our journey together, we have learned a few important things about spiritual growth. First, we have learned that spirituality is measured by outcomes, not by inputs.

The question of how good a Christian you are is directly tied to how closely you resemble Jesus Christ. Put aside everything you know, everything you've accomplished, every position or title you have, and everything others imagine you to be. Put it all aside for a moment and ask yourself, "How spiritual am I really? And how would I know?" *SoulShift* is designed to help answer that question. So, we're not asking if you belong to a small group or if you've been discipled or sanctified or whether you can speak in tongues. We're not asking if you've been to the mission field or inner-city mission. We're not merely concerned with whether you go to church or are a member there. Certainly, these and other spiritual actions are a good thing. If none are present in your life, then there is a problem. But just keeping score on spiritual activities is hollow. When you reach heaven, Jesus will not say, "Well, my friend, I see here in my record book that you've been alone with God seventy times seven, therefore, thou shalt enter into my kingdom."

Second, Jesus wants to see the results of your spiritual activity. The fundamental change for us has been this: We plan inputs, but we measure only outcomes. Inputs (such as disciplines, sacraments, service, worship, commitments) still matter, because they sometimes produce results in our lives. They grow grace in us. But when it comes to sizing up our spirituality, we measure only outcomes.

We've gone from measuring the times you've attended small group or Sunday school class (an input) to measuring the impact of those groups upon your testimony (an outcome). It still matters if you make a commitment or become baptized. We still count that. But the proof of the input is in the outcome. It matters even more if, a year later, the baptized one is in vibrant fellowship with the body (Me to We) or whether he or she has begun the practice of tithing (Consumer to Steward). It matters if someone has a routine day alone with God, but it matters more that this routine has made him or her more sensitive to God's voice (Ask to Listen). It matters that people are still coming to church, but it matters more that they are now volunteering for the children's ministry (Sheep to Shepherd) or participating in a mission trip or working at the community center (Me to You) for the first time.

It's harder to measure these numbers because, in our culture, people value other numbers, such as attendance and offerings. These may be valuable overall indicators, but they don't tell you one lick about how many transformed people are in one place. In addition and with greater importance, we are learning to look for outcomes that are closer to the heart of our spiritual lives.

Rather than focusing only on how many people have made a commitment for Christ or a profession of faith (though we still ask), we want to know what difference their faith actually makes in their decisions, entertainment, or relationships. Instead of defining the spiritual indicators that can measured by a calculator, we are learning to ask the kind of questions that can only be measured by the Spirit and with a story. We now ask, "How has God moved you, this year, from being a Slave toward being a Child?" or "How has God taught you to see more of the Unseen, eternal things around you in the past year?" This changes everything because it means that the most spiritual among us are not those with the deepest thoughts or the longest attendance history. The most spiritual are those who reflect, with ever-increasing clarity, the qualities of Jesus Christ. They are those who are shifting, even in their later years, to become more like our beautiful Savior.

In this book, we have learned about seven specific changes, or shifts, that we must make in our journey toward becoming more like Christ. We defined the goal, something 80 percent of Christians in the church have never done. Sometimes the vision of it alone is enough to pull us into starting new things and making the necessary changes. But just in case that wasn't enough, we took each one of the seven shifts apart, showing how they are not only called for in the Bible, but also actually possible through a series of practical steps. Now, when we start to pray for our own spiritual growth or when we assess it with others in our community, we have the language to talk about it. We have new targets that look different in every age but are the same at their core.

Third, we've seen how these shifts can be encouraged through a series of steps taken on our part. While it is true that only God can transform us, he will not do so without our compliance. He is not a cosmic puppet master who shifts our souls against our will.

No, the way to spiritual growth is to listen to the discontent that God has put into our souls and to cooperate with the Holy Spirit by doing things we have never done before (spiritual disciplines) with people we have never met before (coaches and community) around conversations we have never had before (key convos).

But what about those who, like the waddling residents of Duckville, listen frequently to sermons about flying but still waddle home — as earthbound as ever? What becomes of them? Have you ever noticed that people who get stuck in life rarely get unstuck? They just settle. They compromise. They decide to not be so hard on themselves. Then they look around and, sure enough, just about everyone else is the same, and so they concede that this must be the new normal. But those who get unstuck push on. They refuse to compromise. They define spirituality by the life of Christ, not by the average Christian in their church, and so they are not content "until Christ is formed" in them (Gal. 4:19). Believe it or not, spiritual people get stuck like everyone else. They have seasons in their lives when nothing much is happening, when their energy is low, when they are vulnerable to old scars and sins they should be long over by now. But the difference is that they never stay stuck. They move on. So even when they get stuck again (and they will), they will be further down the road than those who just settled down.

❦

People who live in the northern states know what it means to get stuck. Winters can be hard up there. When a nor'easter (a cold blast from the northeast) comes blowing in, you can forget it. In New England, it causes some of the most intense, perfect storms you can imagine. In the Great Lake states, storms can drop a half-foot of snow on you every hour. In some states, people go inside and pull the shades. Here in Indiana, they cancel church and school and fold up the streets. In Michigan, where I (Steve) was born, they don't let the snow stop them. They take ten miles per hour off their speed and drive wherever they want. Actually, they're playing it safe. Up in Canada, they don't even take off the ten miles per hour.

Invariably, some people will lose control of their cars and get stuck in the ditch. You can see their cars along the highway, abandoned and frosted over. Some of them try to dig themselves out, but only a few will succeed. Most will not. Frustrated that they don't have a winch to pull themselves out, or four-wheel drive, or a big truck, they feel ill-equipped to get unstuck. They'll try for a few moments, but when it appears that it is not going to be easy, they'll walk away.

Have you ever seen someone stuck spiritually? It's very similar. They try for a while to get unstuck. Then it appears that the Christian life is going to be harder than they thought, and they walk away. Not because they aren't serious but, in part, because change is so hard. Like the motorists in the snow bank, they don't feel equipped to get out of the ditch.

Maybe you've been a little stuck yourself. If so, it isn't your fault. Or if it is, you didn't do it on purpose. You're not a bad Christian. You aren't lazy. You're not two-faced. In most cases, getting stuck just happens. It's how all of us on the spiritual journey will end up if we do not take precautions.

Have you ever heard of entropy? It's a fundamental law built into the universe. You've seen it, for sure, even if you didn't know what it was. The law of entropy (or the second law of thermodynamics) says that things wind down, not up. They go from order to disorder. Spin a top, and seconds later, it will be spinning slower, not faster. It will slow down, under the law of entropy, and topple over. Left to themselves, things fall apart, not together. Our bodies grow weaker, not stronger with age. Unattended gardens run to weeds, not to flowers. That's the effect of entropy.

There is such a thing as soul entropy too. Left to ourselves, our spiritual lives will get worse, not better. Our best intentions will run to weeds. All of the momentum we felt in the "hour we first believed" will gradually grind to a halt, and then topple over, and we will get stuck. Usually, getting stuck in soul entropy is not a decision we make, nor even the effect of a hundred little decisions. It is the effect of time itself against our most noble aspirations. Devotions get boring. Community grows stale. Church gets predictable. This whole campaign to shift our souls might go off with a bang, but soon after, it will not be as fun anymore. We will get stuck. In fact, many of us begin our Christian lives with high and lofty dreams only to discover that this Christian life is harder than we thought.

We confuse the meaning of *grace* with *easy* and conclude that, since we are saved by grace, the rest should come easy. When it doesn't, we get discouraged and walk away. "The Christian ideal has not been tried and found wanting," G. K. Chesterton said. "It has been found difficult; and left untried."[6] I (Steve) thought of that a few weeks ago while a student at a Christian university was telling me how hard it was for him to be a Christian. "I can't do it anymore," he said. "I guess I'm not cut out for this 'Christian' thing. It's just too hard." He is stuck. Something has gone wrong.

Why does this happen? From our experiences, there are two reasons. Both are subtle, yet powerful forces that pull us off track. One is when something comes up, and the other is when something goes wrong. These are two categories of distractions, and we must stay alert for both.

When something comes up, we run into something that we didn't plan on and it distracts us from the thing we have set out to do. We chase new opportunities in our work. We sign up for graduate studies. We adopt a child from a Third World country. We accept a promotion. Our son makes the traveling soccer team. Our daughter announces her engagement. None of these things are bad. In fact, they're all good. But all of them take time and energy. And before we know it, our focus is blurred. Stuff happens, and we forget to shift in the midst of it. We still love God, but we are unable to find him in these circumstances, so he becomes increasingly irrelevant, marginalized to the "spiritual life." Things we once considered important are pushed out by what Charles Hummel called "the tyranny of the urgent."[7] That's what happens when something comes up.

But when something goes wrong, we are confronted with a problem, and we have no choice but to give it our full attention. We are compelled by circumstances or by those in power over us, and we do whatever we must in order to survive. A son is diagnosed with a learning disorder. Your marriage hits the rocks. A retirement fund crashes. You get transferred to another city. A husband is called up for active duty.

Soon, we are surrounded by things that do not remind us very much of God. We hardly think of him at all. Something has gone wrong. Quite often, it is not the thing itself that hurls us into the ditch, but the manner in which we react to it. It is the way we protect ourselves or the way we try to control the situation. Gradually, we hide in our pride, our discontent, our fear, or any number of soul diseases. Then, little by little, these habits erode our confidence and joy. All at once, we awaken to find that we are stuck in our spiritual lives.

Instead of the wonderful outcomes of a shifted heart, we end up only doing the habits, or inputs, with almost nothing to show for it. Instead of selflessness, we remain selfish. Instead of freedom, we stay in patterns of bondage. Instead of responsibility, we choose to consume our way through life. Instead of influencing others to follow Christ, we follow the crowd. This is what it looks like to have your soul stuck in the ditch.

If you're stuck, here's what to do. First, relax. Don't panic. Keep at it, but take it easy. When some people get stuck, they punch down the accelerator too fast and furiously. They get nervous ("I can't afford to be stuck!") or they get scared ("What will other people think of me if they see me stuck?") or they get down on themselves ("What did I do wrong to get stuck?"). They throw themselves into a flurry of activity, thinking they can blast themselves out by going faster. But they end up only spinning their wheels, and a little while later they are just as stuck as ever, only they are more tired and apt to walk away. The more you spin your wheels, the more slippery the ditch becomes.

So if you get stuck in your spiritual life, and you almost certainly will, don't panic. Don't blame other people. Don't pick on yourself. Don't pretend that you don't care. Don't jump churches. Don't experiment with new religions. Don't make rash promises you can't keep. And above all, don't compare yourself with other Christians who seem, to you, not to be stuck. It is essential, right here, that you remember how you got started in the first place.

Remember that you were drawn by the Holy Spirit into this beautiful, if frustrating, friendship with Jesus Christ. You did not become a Christian all on your own, and you will not become a better one all on your own. The God who loves you will not let you go that easily. He will pursue you, compel you, hold you, and wait for you, even when it seems like he is doing nothing. He wants this more than you do. Besides, you will learn over time that you grow spiritually the way you grow physically. It is not all at once; you grow in spurts, during different seasons of your life. Getting stronger spiritually is not like body building (sorry, Mr. Atlas), where you increase your strength a little every day and mostly through your own hard work. Rather, your seasons of spiritual growth are often preceded by periods of frustration, failure, and anxiety. These unresolved conflicts are the growing pains of your soul, and they are often accompanied by a sudden increase in your appetite for the Word of God, or the fellowship of the church, or a deeper friendship with Jesus Christ. By feeding these natural desires, implanted as they are by the Holy Spirit, you are enabling God to shift your soul.

So when you first notice that you're stuck, instead of spinning your wheels with all sorts of new activity, simply pray and tell God that you're stuck. Maybe it's right now. Maybe you should stop reading, right here, and tell God that you are tired, that you feel nothing, that you can't get your soul started again, and that you don't know what to do. Pray as Teresa of Avila once prayed, "Lord, I do not love you. I do not even want to love you, but I want to want to love you. Amen."[8]

Second, stay active. This may sound like a contradiction, because we first told you to relax and now we're telling you to stay active. Think of it like this: When you get stuck, you can't do everything (so relax), but you must do something (so stay active). Too many people just quit. They abandon their cars, or worse, they stay in them and stare out the windshield, like they do in church.

When I (Steve) was a young pastor, I used to visit the people in my community who hadn't been in church for a while. I would show up on their porch and try to talk to them about their spiritual lives, but most of these conversations went nowhere. These were former members, sometimes former elders, who were once very active in the church but, through a series of circumstances, had fallen out of fellowship and were now staying home every Sunday. I was worried about their spiritual lives. They were inactive. But over the years, I have come to grieve as much those who are in the church and inactive, as I do those who are out of it. They have found the Christian life to be as difficult for them as it was for the others who left the church, and so they have left the Christian life untried. But they have never left the church.

You've seen them, too, haven't you? Their stories are stale, their conversations shallow, and their answers trite. Their lives do not bear fruit. They have no spirit of adventure. They are inactive, but not because they are content. Rather, they are stuck. Buried under something that has come up or gone wrong, they have never gotten back to the level of their first love for Christ. Sometimes they get critical of what is happening in their church. No longer able to perform, and yet never good enough to coach, they can at least vote on all that is happening in their church, so they become the consummate Christian consumer. Their new role is to critique the sermons, music, and programs—all the stuff on Sunday mornings you can show up to and attend. They are stuck, but they have never left the church. They simply stare out the windshield every Sunday morning.

If you are one of them, in the name of our Lord, don't quit and remain stuck. Don't walk away. Don't hunker down. Stay in the struggle. Stay in the fellowship of believers. Keep reading the Word of God, not only on Sundays but in between. Keep practicing your current spiritual disciplines. Stay accountable to the others in your group. Keep confessing your sins to your elders or to your spiritual advisor. Keep taking the sacrament, as often as they serve it in your church. And while you do this, pray for another growth spurt. To be sure, all this activity must not be confused with progress, but progress cannot be separated from this activity. "The power of God," said A. W. Tozer, "comes only when it is called out by the plow."[9]

Third, find traction. In the winter states, travelers who have been stuck often carry extra equipment to help give them traction the next time. They pack shovels, sand, chains, carpet, gravel, and just about anything else in their cars so they can throw it under the tire that is stuck. They try to get traction in the place where they were only spinning before.

When you become stuck, if your soul has not really shifted in a while, consider doing something new to give yourself traction. While you must not throw yourself into a flurry of activity, you might consider doing one new thing in your spiritual life that you think is connected to the reason you are stuck. For instance, if you're stuck because you are bored with your religion, then consider a new adventure—like a short-term mission trip or volunteering for a new ministry in your church—that is far outside your comfort zone. If you are struggling with the same old sin, then consider seeking out a spiritual coach who will mentor you and act as an accountability partner. If you are distracted by a lot of minutia in your life, then consider taking on a couple new disciplines that will force you to focus.

In one group I (Steve) was in, we listed about twenty spiritual disciplines and challenged each other to select from the list two that we were not already using. Then we met every other week to ask each other how it was going and what difference the discipline was making in our lives. The secret to finding traction in your spiritual life is to diagnose, with the help of another person (your pastor, counselor, or coach), the reason you became stuck. Then, develop a new practice in your life that counters it. Very soon, you will find yourself beginning to move again.

Finally, go slow. People who have never been stuck often make the mistake of trying to bust out of their gridlock in a single bound. But all that does is eliminate the traction they had a moment ago. The way out is slow. It can be frustrating and fraught with failure. But those who get unstuck are the ones who keep trying. Often it's an even lower gear with a slower spiritual torque that becomes the answer to getting unstuck.

If you are stuck in your spiritual life, you are probably more than one revival away from getting unstuck. Listening to one good sermon or reading a book (yes, even this one) will not change your predicament. So, if you're working on a SoulShift and it is not coming easily, don't expect to master it in a month. Give yourself time. Reread the chapters on the shift that is difficult for you and map out a strategy for implementing the advice. If you're trying to rid yourself of a certain sin, you cannot throw it out the upstairs window. You must coax it down the stairs a step at a time. Put into place the people and the disciplines necessary for a SoulShift to occur and then be patient. Measure your progress by the year, not by the day. And by all means, measure your progress.

The great, British evangelist John Wesley preached a sermon called, "Satan's Devices" (they had some pretty direct sermon titles back in the day). Wesley preached his heart out to his listeners, more than likely a crowd of regular Joe coal miners in a field, with Wesley on top of a tree-stump turned pulpit. He said, "The grand device of Satan [is] to destroy the first work of God in the soul . . . by our expectation of that greater work."[10] The way to fight back, said Wesley, was to constantly remind ourselves of the hope that even in our frustration, our humility and joy are increased as we wait for the day when God finally transforms our souls. By this, "the greater that change is which remains to be wrought in your soul, the more may you triumph in the Lord, and rejoice in the God of your salvation, who hath done so great things for you already."[11]

In our staff meetings, we have developed a habit of interrupting our meetings periodically with stories of how God is shifting our souls. We will mention a particular SoulShift and then go around the table asking, "Where have you seen this shift happening? Who has been making these kinds of changes in their life?" Then we all share our stories and the staff celebrates the progress God has given us. In another meeting, we gathered one hundred of our key leaders into a large room and posted the seven shifts, like stations, along the walls. We then asked our leaders to go stand under the SoulShift that God has been pressing upon them lately. Once the little groups of fifteen or twenty had formed, we asked them to tell others in their circle what God had been doing to encourage that shift in their lives. It was amazing to see how God was shifting all of us, in his way and in his time, to become more like Christ.

The shifts are a way to intentionally get your soul into gear and grow like never before. Of course, you are not shifting alone. God is doing this in you. When others meet the new you, they may even thank you, appreciating the changes you've made. Always remember that God alone deserves the praise. He is the one who makes the great exchange in your soul. The psalmist said, "You turned my wailing into dancing; you removed my sackcloth and clothed me with joy" (Ps. 30:11 TNIV). Eugene Peterson translates this psalm wonderfully—you can make it your prayer, "You did it: you changed wild lament into whirling dance; you ripped off my black mourning band and decked me with wildflowers. I'm about to burst with song; I can't keep quiet about you. God, my God, I can't thank you enough" (Ps. 30:11–12 MSG).

God is in the business of helping you trade in what is broken and stuck and replacing it with what is beautiful. All the flightless ducks of Duckville can rejoice, for in his Spirit, we truly learn to spread our wings and fly.

EPILOGUE

GOD'S GARAGE

Marv invited me (Steve) to come over to his garage where he said he was hiding a gem. Marv loves to restore old cars. It is not because he hates new cars; he's just drawn toward the classic ones. On the walk from the house to the garage, he boasted about his 1964 Pontiac GTO. It was fire-truck red, he told me, and would go from zero to sixty in a few seconds. "Just wait until you see it," he boasted.

When Marv opened the door, I saw something quite different. There on the floor was his red-hot GTO in a thousand pieces, each one carefully disassembled by him and set into groups, awaiting its day with Marv. I couldn't believe he had put a bunch of money into this! It looked like a junkyard selection of parts.

On the wall, however, was a photo of the potential these parts had: a 1964 Pontiac GTO, fire-truck red, completely restored to its original condition.

As we surveyed the parts, he said, "What do you think?"

"Well, I'm speechless."

The look on my face gave me away. This was no classic. This was not even a car. It was a piece of junk—in fact, thousands of pieces of junk.

Before I could work up the nerve to ask him what he paid for this, Marv started going from one part to another, calling each piece by name, and telling me how he was going to put them together to create, or actually to re-create, something I would recognize and admire in the end. He described a car just as perfect as the picture on the wall.

"How long have you been working on this?" I asked.

"A long time," he said, "but I'm in no hurry. I work on it a little here and there, whenever I have time. It's coming along."

Though I could not see why at that moment, Marv was immensely proud of his classic car, broken to smithereens as it was. He was proud of it even though he was very aware of its current condition—in fact, he was far more aware than I was. He told me what was wrong with certain parts I didn't even notice were there. And what's more, in his mind, he knew the potential of all those pieces put together. He had a mental picture of what that clunker would look like, and that's why he paid more for it than it was worth. That's why he bragged about it all the way to the garage, speaking of its future as if it had already happened. Its future is why he worked so hard on it every time he walked in that garage. Noticing every flaw, he would go after it with a vengeance—not because he was mad at the car for being broken, but because he loved it and knew its true potential. The picture on the wall reminded him of that future dream.

What's more, he would also be reminded of its past. For the future of any classic is only its past. In that sense, Marv was never creating something new, something previously unheard of, so much as he was restoring what was lost. When he is done, it will not be an innovation—but it will be an original, a classic. And there is not just one kind of classic, but hundreds. To convert his 1964 Pontiac GTO into a 1967 Ford Mustang would be not only impossible, but also foolish. His classic is unique. Its future potential is beautiful.

So is yours.

Your potential is beautiful beyond your dreams. Perhaps God posts a picture on his wall of what you will look like once he has finished restoring you. He brags about you to the angels, "Have you noticed my servant? No one quite like him on earth—he's a unique gem!" He might say, "Have you seen my child doing all of this for me lately? She's a classic for sure." And now that I think of it, he also paid more to get you and me than we were worth.

But you're not fully restored yet. The angels may wonder why he paid so much for you. Your life, as it is, may be in chaos at times. But he enters the garage of your soul, going after sin with a vengeance—not merely because he is mad at your sinning. He works so hard because he knows it is inconsistent with the picture of your future that he has on his wall. He longs to shift your soul closer to the original condition he created. He wants to restore your soul. It's time to let him.

Not that I have already obtained all this, or have already been made perfect, but I press on to take hold of that for which Christ Jesus took hold of me. (Phil. 3:12)

In his kindness God called you to share in his eternal glory by means of Christ Jesus. So after you have suffered a little while, he will restore, support, and strengthen you, and he will place you on a firm foundation. (1 Pet. 5:10 NLT)

NOTES

PREFACE

1. Bill Tancer, *Click: What Millions of People Are Doing Online and Why It Matters* (New York: Hyperion Books, 2008), 74.

2. Ibid., 79.

3. Greg Ogden, *Transforming Discipleship: Making Disciples a Few at a Time* (Downers Grove, Ill.: InterVarsity Press, 2003), 27.

4. George Barna, *Growing True Disciples: New Strategies for Producing Genuine Followers of Christ* (Colorado Springs: WaterBrook Press, 2001), 36–37.

5. Ibid., 46.

6. Ibid., 47.

7. Ibid.

INTRODUCTION

1. Bill Tancer, *Click: What Millions of People Are Doing Online and Why It Matters* (New York: Hyperion Books, 2008), 71.

CHAPTER 1

1. "The KJV New Testament Greek Lexicon," s.v. "Hamartia," accessed September 1, 2010, http://www.biblestudytools.com/lexicon/greek/kjv/ hamartia.html.
2. "St. Francis of Assisi Quotes," accessed September 1, 2010, http://thinkexist.com/quotes/st._francis_of_assisi/.

CHAPTER 2

1. George MacDonald, *Unspoken Sermons: Series I, II, and III* (n.p.: CreateSpace, 2009), 183.
2. Kenneth E. Bailey, *Poet and Peasant and Through Peasant Eyes: A Literary-Cultural Approach to the Parables in Luke*, combined ed. (Grand Rapids, Mich.: Eerdmans, 1983), 181.
3. Henri J. M. Nouwen, *The Return of the Prodigal Son: A Story of Homecoming* (New York: Doubleday, 1994), 53.
4. Ibid.
5. Dennis F. Kinlaw, *Let's Start with Jesus: A New Way of Doing Theology* (Grand Rapids, Mich.: Zondervan, 2005), 66.

CHAPTER 3

1. Sarah Meyer, telephone interview with David Drury, April 5, 2010.
2. Tom Wright, *John for Everyone, Chapters 11–21* (Louisville, Ky.: Westminster John Knox Press, 2004), 153–154.
3. John Ortberg, *Faith and Doubt* (Grand Rapids, Mich.: Zondervan, 2008), 16.
4. "Thornton Wilder Quotes," accessed September 2, 2010, http://thinkexist.com/quotes/thornton_wilder/.
5. Yann Martel, *The Life of Pi* (New York: Harcourt, 2001), 28.

6. Thomas Merton, *Life and Holiness* (New York: Doubleday, 1996), 76.

7. Ortberg, *Faith and Doubt*, 24–25.

CHAPTER 4

1. "Major League Eating," accessed September 3, 2010, http://www.ifoce.com/rankings.php.

2. Pablo S. Torre, "Coney Island Contender: Chestnut Fails in Quest to Become Hot Dog-Eating Champ," *Sports Illustrated* (July 5, 2006), accessed May 19, 2010, http://sportsillustrated.cnn.com/2006/sioncampus/07/05/nathans.hotdog/index.html.

3. Ibid.

4. "Major League Eating Records," accessed May 19, 2010, http://www.ifoce.com/records.php.

5. "Farm Animal Statistics: Meat Consumption," accessed May 19, 2010, http://www.humanesociety.org/news/resources/research/stats_meat_consumption.html.

6. Ronald J. Sider, *Rich Christians in an Age of Hunger: Moving from Affluence to Generosity* (Nashville: Thomas Nelson, 2005), 23.

7. "Rasheed Wallace and Flip Saunders' Strained Relationship," accessed June 23, 1010, http://www.detroitbadboys.com/2007/1/11/1214991/rasheed-wallace-and-flip-saunders.

8. Skye Jethani, *The Divine Commodity: Discovering a Faith Beyond Consumer Christianity* (Grand Rapids, Mich.: Zondervan, 2009), 11.

9. Ibid., 20.

10. Howard Dayton, *Your Money Counts: The Biblical Guide to Earning, Spending, Saving, Investing, Giving, and Getting Out of Debt* (Carol Stream, Ill.: Tyndale, 1996), 2.

11. For more on these ideas, see Barry Schwartz, *The Paradox of Choice: Why More Is Less* (New York: Harper Collins, 2004).

12. Wesley K. Willmer and Martyn Smith, *God and Your Stuff: The Vital Link Between Your Possessions and Your Soul* (Colorado Springs: NavPress, 2002), 33–34.

CHAPTER 5

1. John Faherty, "After 42 Years, Woman Hears for First Time," *The Arizona Republic* (August 30, 2006), accessed June 3, 2010,http://www.first coastnews.com/news/health/newsarticle.aspx?ref=rss&storyid= 63812.

2. In fact, Jesus repeats this, in so many words, ten times in his last lecture to the disciples (John 13:33, 36; 14:2, 12, 28; 16:5, 7, 10, 16, 28). This is clearly the most important theme in what is often called the Olivet Discourse.

3. Fred B. Craddock, *Preaching* (Nashville: Abingdon, 1985), 52.

4. Henri J. M. Nouwen, *Spiritual Direction: Wisdom for the Long Walk of Faith*, eds. Michael J. Christensen and Rebecca Laird (New York: HarperCollins, 2006), 88.

5. As told by Dennis Jackson in his "Ordinary Day" sermon delivered to Spring Lake Wesleyan Church on October 9, 2005.

CHAPTER 6

1. Douglas K. Stuart, *The New American Commentary* (Nashville: Broadman & Holman, 2006), 95.

2. Alan Cole, *Exodus*, Tyndale Old Testament Commentary Series (Downers Grove, Ill.: InterVarsity Press, 1973), 59.

3. George Barna reports that "fewer than one out of every [twenty] pastors believes he/she has the spiritual gift of leadership" in *The Habits of Highly Effective Churches: Being Strategic in Your God-Given Ministry* (Ventura, Calif.: Regal Books, 1999), 31.

4. Max Lucado, *A Gentle Thunder: Hearing God Through the Storm* (Nashville: Thomas Nelson, 1995), 73.

5. Ibid., 74.

CHAPTER 7

1. Adam Hochschild, *Bury the Chains: Prophets and Rebels in the Fight to Free an Empire's Slaves* (New York: Houghton Mifflin, 2005), 131.

For other information, see John Newton, *Thoughts Upon the African Slave Trade* (Ithaca, N.Y.: Cornell University Library, 1788).

2. Kevin Bales, *Disposable People: New Slavery in the Global Economy* (Berkeley: University of California Press, 1999), 23.

3. Leonard Sweet, "From Podiums and Pulpits to the Pew: Authorial Authority in a Google World" (Kenote Speech, Indianapolis Christian Writers' Conference, Fishers, Ind., November 6, 2009).

4. Facebook search on "I talk about myself too much," accessed September 22, 2010, http://www.Facebook.com.

5. Philip Langdon, *A Better Place to Live: Reshaping the American Suburb* (Amherst: University of Massachusetts Press, 1997), 1.

6. John L. Locke, *Why We Don't Talk to Each Other Anymore: The De-Voicing of Society* (New York: Simon & Schuster, 1999), 132.

7. Ibid., 133.

8. Ibid.

9. Paul Brand and Philip Yancey, *Fearfully and Wonderfully Made: A Surgeon Looks at the Human & Spiritual Body* (Grand Rapids, Mich.: Zondervan, 1980), 20.

10. Peter Block, *Community: The Structure of Belonging* (San Francisco: Berrett-Koehler, 2008), 63.

11. Paul said, "God has arranged the parts in the body, every one of them, *just as he wanted them to be*" (1 Cor. 12:18, emphasis added).

12. Desmond Tutu, *God Has a Dream: A Vision of Hope for Our Time* (New York: Doubleday, 2004), 26.

13. Larry Chang, *Wisdom for the Soul: Five Millennia of Prescriptions for Spiritual Healing* (Washington, D.C.: Gnosophia, 2006), 162.

14. Anne Lamott, *Traveling Mercies: Some Thoughts on Faith* (New York: Pantheon, 1999), 55.

CHAPTER 8

1. Disciplines of Abstinence are those in which you don't do something—removing an element of life—in order to focus on God and his

desires for you. The inspiration for this list comes from the chapters in part one of Keith Drury, *With Unveiled Faces: Experience Intimacy with God Through Spiritual Disciplines* (Indianapolis, Ind.: Wesleyan Publishing House, 2005), 11–67.

2. Disciplines of Action are those in which you do something special—adding an element to life—in order to focus on God and his desires for you. The chapters in part two of Drury's *With Unveiled Faces* inspire this list (68–148).

3. Disciplines of Association are those in which you do something in the community of Christ—adding community to your life—in order to focus on God and his desires for you. We have drawn inspiration for this list from Keith Drury, *There Is No I in Church* (Indianapolis, Ind.: Wesleyan Publishing House, 2006). This book challenges us to move beyond individual spirituality to the corporate disciplines of the church.

CHAPTER 9

1. George Barna, *Revolution* (Carol Stream, Ill.: Tyndale House, 2005), 32.
2. Ibid., 34.
3. — — —, *Growing True Disciples: New Strategies for Producing Genuine Followers of Christ* (Colorado Springs: WaterBrook Press, 2001), 59.
4. Ibid., 74.
5. Barna, *Revolution*, 34.
6. G. K. Chesterton, *What's Wrong with the World* (n.p.: CreateSpace, 2009), 18.
7. Charles E. Hummel, *Tyranny of the Urgent!* (Downers Grove, Ill.: InterVarsity Press, 1994).
8. Tim Clinton and Joshua Straub, *God Attachment: Why You Believe, Act, and Feel the Way You Do About God* (New York: Simon & Schuster, 2010), 28.

9. A. W. Tozer, *Paths to Power* (Camp Hill, Pa.: Christian Publications, 1992), 23.

10. John Wesley, "Satan's Devices," *The Works of John Wesley*, 3rd ed. (Kansas City, Mo.: Beacon Hill, 1979), VI: 33.

11. Ibid., 40.

Encourage genuine change in your church like never before!

SoulShift Church Resource Kit

by Steve DeNeff and David Drury

SoulShift is an eight-week journey that challenges your congregation to experience seven key shifts—life changes that God's Spirit can bring about in hearts, minds, and behaviors. The SoulShift Church Resource Kit contains everything your church leadership needs to create an all-church transformation experience, moving the congregation toward a deeper, Spirit-driven formation.

This kit is packed with tested-in-the-church resources that will help you launch and lead a two-month SoulShift quest.

- Copy of *SoulShift: The Measure of a Life Transformed*
- *Strategic Planning Guide*
- Sermon Introductions DVD-ROM
- 3 Group Study DVDs
- Resources CD-ROM
- Unlimited access for SoulShift leaders to online resources, including all of the contents of the CD-ROM and much more at www.oursoulshift.com
- 5 copies of *SoulShift Magazine*

Follow-Up Studies for Each Shift

ISBN: 978-0-89827-480-6

ISBN: 978-0-89827-477-6

ISBN: 978-0-89827-482-0

God wants to change how you live by changing who you are. And while that doesn't mean he is out to rewrite your identity, it does mean his plan is for you to be a new creation.

In this series of Bible studies based on *SoulShift: The Measure of a Life Transformed*, you will find a powerful and practical approach to spiritual formation that goes beyond spiritual disciplines to focus on who you are becoming in Christ.

Each four-week study provides Scripture readings, thought-provoking questions for personal reflection, and discussion questions for group exploration.

Also Available—
- *Consumer to Steward: Cultivating a Generous Spirit*
  ISBN: 978-0-89827-479-0
- *Ask to Listen: Discerning the Voice of God*
  ISBN: 978-0-89827-481-3
- *Sheep to Shepherd: Guiding Others toward Maturity in Christ*
  ISBN: 978-0-89827-478-3
- *Me to We: Uniting with the Church Community*
  ISBN: 978-0-89827-483-7

For more about
SoulShift and additional
resources, go to
www.oursoulshift.com.

wesleyan
publishing
house

www.wesleyan.org/wph
1.800.493.7539